THE STATE
of the
Republic

HOW THE MISADVENTURES OF U.S.
POLICY SINCE WWII HAVE LED TO THE
QUAGMIRE OF TODAY'S ECONOMIC, SOCIAL
AND POLITICAL DISAPPOINTMENTS

HARRY GAEL MICHAELS

20Twenty
Literary Group

The State of the Republic
Copyright © 2024 by Harry Gael Michaels

ISBN
978-1-961250-64-2 (Paperback)
978-1-961250-65-9 (eBook)
978-1-961250-63-5 (Hardcover)

Table of Contents

Table of Contents

Letter of Appeal to the People of the
United States of America

"These are times that try men's souls"
Thomas Paine, 1775.

The intention of this letter is to promote a renewed spirit of goodwill and re-dedication to the intentions of our foresightful forefathers who gave us a Democratic society with values of liberty, freedom, justice and a pursuit of happiness for all within the context of the responsibility that is, and which responsibility is eternally hinged to those ideals—since responsibility is the keystone of this great edifice and without it we founder in a morass of self-interest and degeneration. When the Declaration of Independence was finally signed someone asked Benjamin Franklin; "Now what do we have?" Franklin responded, "We have a democratic republic, if you can keep it."

I am a 93year old with a working background in school psychology and juvenile probation and I have seen many struggles and crises in modern American history as well as the emergence of successful resolutions, however, we are, it seems to me, at a point in our history that could determine our destiny as a thriving democracy or a decaying autocracy.

More and more on the news I hear the pleas for an end to the vicious polarization of our people and a "reknitting" of community and civic sentiment of our social patterns. Every day, now, and for the past many years since the electrifying tragedy at Columbine high school in April of 1999, we have witnessed not only the dissolute and senseless shooting and killing of innocent men, women and children because of an unqualified and unrestrained interpretation of the 2nd amendment to our Constitution but also a schismatic and destructive polarization of our political system of government—which some say could lead to civil war. It appears to this writer that there is an element in this society that is so frightened by the apparent disorder, confusion, and disarray among our governmental leaders that they are clamoring for an autocratic (and seemingly powerful leader such as Donald Trump) who they perceive as re-establishing order, security and (greatness) to America. With reference to the former President of the United States, Donald J. Trump, what concerns me the most is not so much the beneficial effects he might have on enriching our economy and even the fortunes of the wealthy and those in great financial power, but his extreme self-serving approach to the law and the Constitution of the United States. I, for one, find it too difficult to put much trust or confidence in such a person and why would I want to follow a leader who I could not trust to abide by the same laws as the one's I must follow.

It appears we have entered a critical period in which the ideals of democracy or a digression into autocracy are in contention for ascendency in the United States of America. We are seeing a voracious aggression by elements of those who would dictate our destiny and rape our economic structure with a lust for power, greed, and self-interest.

There is a pall hanging over our nation which is permeating the social atmosphere resulting in an inordinate number of suicides even among children. Anxiety, depression, rage and hopelessness in a society like ours, especially in our young people, cannot be tolerated without its destruction.

My appeal is to those, however, who understand the dire urgency of moving our Ship of State back on a more viable course and I beseech those enlightened people of good will who recognize the problem clearly to summon greater will and determination to right the wrongs and think of inspiring the youth and progeny of this great Country with hope and purpose by addressing the origins of our disarray and focusing on:

- Early childhood education with professional behavioral observation and school readiness evaluations,
- Employing the functional elderly in part-time useful positions in the schools to not waste their acquired skills and knowledge.
- Relating the truth to our youth (as best we understand it) about our history, civic structures, and culture.
- To be specific; mental health services are critically important these days as an adjunct to elementary, junior high and high school education and would be the intervention and

establishment of group counseling starting in the primary elementary grades for the socially isolated because social isolation is a trigger for destructive impulses—either toward the self or outwardly toward the public at large. Also, any form of bullying or intimidation whether in the schools or on the internet must be absolutely zeroed out.

- Special training for those who wish to enter education and political or public service with emphasis on the importance of carrying the banner of ethics and honor with integrity, perspicacity, and discernment.

At the writing of this letter we have seen, once again, the outright murder of 19 elementary school children and two of their teachers in a small town in Texas by an enraged 18year old with a military style rapid fire assault weapon designed for combat in a field of battle. At 18 he was able to purchase such a weapon, however, at his age he was not considered old enough to buy a hand gun or alcohol or cigarettes. Where is our legislative perspicacity?

We might ask ourselves why we have 8 times more gun homicides than Canada, 50 times more than Germany, 100 times more than England and 250 times more than Japan per 100,000 residents. We have about half the guns in the world. Other countries have more effective gun controls. Why not this Country? Why, don't we at least require all gun owners to be registered, licensed and tested for competency like we do for having an automobile? Having a license to drive an automobile is considered a privilege not a right as ought to be the issue in owning of a firearm.

We might ask ourselves why we permit our political leaders in Washington to exercise power contrary to the will of a 90-percent majority of Americans over the issue of establishing effective gun control? Should the NRA have so much power and influence over the administration of the laws that we as a nation abide by?

We might consider a re-visitation of the 2nd Amendment to the Constitution because if one studies the reason for its original adoption, we may see a reason to update it. The original intent of our Founding Fathers in constructing the 2nd Amendment to the Bill of Rights was to avoid a standing army but, at the same time, they felt a need for a well-regulated militia to put down insurrections such as the Shay and Whiskey rebellions over the issue of high taxation, and, also, in restraining black and Indian populations from uprisings and disorder. There were also dis-regulated groups such as the Carolina Regulators and vigilante groups such as the Pennsylvania Paxton Boys. Furthermore, many people lived out on isolated farms and required firearms for protection against renegade outlaws, Indians, wild animals and even British sympathizers. Back in the 18th century having a firearm or two was a necessity for protection and maintaining order. I think too many Americans identify their citizenship and loyalty with the 2nd Amendment as part of a fundamental belief system, however, such an identity seems to cause an unwillingness to adapt to the evolutionary changes that a free democratic society requires. I remember the great film actor Charlton Heston, at an NRA meeting, holding an old Revolutionary rifle over his head and belting out, "From my cold hands." This was his way of dramatically showing the intensity of his identity as an American by means of his loyalty to the 2nd Amendment.

Today, we live in a society of laws, police and sheriff department protection, National Guard, courts and judicial systems and a powerful standing military. There is no need for a "right to bear arms" and, certainly, no need for military assault weapons in the hands of 18year old adolescent boys with known histories of aberrant, anti-social attitudes. It is critical that we address all these problems sensibly and thoughtfully, now. This problem of unbridled criminal disorder against innocent children in school has been growing increasingly since the Columbine event over 23 years ago, therefore, the things I urge Americans to focus on today to mediate out-of-control mass shootings are:

- Possession of any and all automatic and semi-automatic assault rifles that were designed for military combat must be regarded as a felony.
- Require thorough background checks for any purchase of any firearm.
- Require registration, licensing and tests of competency to own or be in possession of a firearm.

- "Red Flag" provisions must be approved to allow for professional intervention at a time of impending crisis.
- Revisit the 2nd Amendment to re-qualify it for conformance with the conditions of American life today.
- At the present at least 2 or 3 of the teacher staff must be equipped and trained with the use of firearms. We have seen in too many past incidences that depending on local public safety is not always reliable and children must be protected by any means possible.

Finally, I wish to close this Letter of Appeal by stating that I claim no final authority in these matters. I only offer the benefit of my personal experience and professional training as a juvenile probation officer in the 60s and then many years as a school psychologist until my retirement. I have kept abreast of the changes over the years, that have led us to where we are today and, in my view, we are in a tumultuous societal, political and economic storm. So, as in any crisis we have an opportunity to make important changes. We must choose wise and compassionate leaders to guide our Ship of State toward calmer seas and brighter horizons. The time is urgent and the time is now.

For a better future.

The two anthems, America the Beautiful and The Star-Spangled Banner, represent the fondest aspirations of the American people and yet they also suggest an internal fugue in the disposition of American National attitude. On the one hand, we aspire to present to the to the world "A shining city on the hill" as was a favorite expression of Ronald Reagan, while on the other, it represents a beleaguered country desperately hanging on to its sovereignty against a mortal threat and extinction through extraordinary gallantry and bravery. It is with this bifurcation of mindfulness that I write this book.

Part I

The Road to Dysfunction and Decline

In the year 1945, historians were suggesting that the coming era would be described as the "Age of Anxiety" because for the first time in human history, the world had to face the possibility of nuclear annihilation. We did not anticipate the anxiety that would pervade this country due to the social/political/economic misadventures of the post WWII era. However, we emerged from WWII as an unequaled world power and confident of controlling the nuclear genie. The United States had decisively won, perhaps, the most significant war in history and then began to reach out to its conquered enemies to help them in their recovery and reconstruction.

At the close of WWII in Europe and the discovery of the suicidal remains of Adolph Hitler and his new bride, Eva Braun, in a bunker near the Reich Chancellery, Germany was in a state of total destruction and collapse. Then in 1948, under the Marshall Plan conceived by General George C. Marshall, President Truman's Secretary of State, C-54 cargo planes from the U.S. were dispatched on a round-the-clock schedule flying into Berlin with vital supplies for the devastated German people and helping them restore their shattered homeland to some semblance of order and recovery, while at Nuremberg, Nazi war criminals were being prosecuted for unspeakable crimes against humanity. It was during this time that the full horror of the death camps came to light. As a result of the Yalta (Feb. 1945) and Potsdam (Aug. 1945) conferences, a decision was made by the allied governments to acquiesce to the Premier of the Soviet Union, Joseph Stalin, and his demands for control of east Berlin and eastern Germany at the end of the war. From there it was rather easy for Stalin to annex the rest of Eastern Europe as well as the tiny countries of Latvia, Estonia and Lithuania.

Other concessions were made as well to Stalin in the Far East. He was given control of the Kuril Islands and South Sakhalin Island north of Japan, the port cities of Darien and Port Arthur as well as control of the Manchurian railway. This was to be his reward for entering the war against Japan six days before the unconditional surrender of the Japanese on the deck of the battleship, Missouri, in Tokyo Bay. As an aside, it is interesting to note that in recent years there have been friendly meetings at some of the Pacific battle sites between veterans of the U.S. as well as those of the

Japanese. A documentary was broadcast on American television over 60 years after the bombing of Pearl Harbor in 1941 in which a veteran Japanese pilot who took part in the attack, was met by a veteran American pilot, at Pearl Harbor on the Memorial of the U.S.S. Arizona, in which they recalled their part in the event— in friendship and good will.

After the Japanese surrender, General Douglas MacArthur set about establishing a new post-war democratic political system in that devastated country and the Emperor Hirohito was no longer regarded as a descendent of the Sun God. Japanese citizens could now look upon his face while they cleaned up the utter devastation and first use of nuclear weapon in the history of warfare and the utter obliteration of Nagasaki and Hiroshima, the first two cities ever to be destroyed by nuclear weapons. Even though MacArthur was a political conservative, most of those working under him were liberal democrats who were following the deceased President Roosevelt's "New Deal." This was in recognition of labor unions and the notion of collective bargaining to settle labor-management differences such as wages, work hours or working conditions. Generally, the New Deal allowed for private enterprise under the guidance of the government.

Back home, returning veterans had begun enjoying their rewards of victory by starting families and continuing their education on the GI Bill. All over America college campuses were bordered by Quonset huts and barrack-type living quarters for married vets and their families. Young kids were now going to college with older veterans and could find themselves sitting next to a war-wise former officer or enlisted man from any branch of the Armed Forces. Adequate housing was quite accessible at a three percent, thirty-year fixed mortgage or less on a VA loan. Things were booming as "Rosie the Riveter" relinquished her job for a returning serviceman and women went back into the home—at least, temporarily. New cars, toasters and refrigerators hit the market and wartime ration stamp books went out in the trash. The price of a Coca Cola was five cents. You could buy a new car for $900.00 dollars and a new house for $9,000.00. The cost of a postage stamp was three cents.

The United Nations Organization was formed in San Francisco in 1945 and its first major challenge was the Korean conflict that began in 1950. Communist-inspired Koreans from the north, who had seen the Communist take-over of China in 1949, launched an all-out attack on the southern provinces of Korea. It was believed that the incursion of North Korea, under the Russian installed Kim Il Sung, into South Korea under the leadership of the American installed Syngman Rhee, a devout Christian and with a Ph.D. in political science from Princeton, could trigger an Armageddon if nuclear weapons were to be used. A plan, therefore, of containment and resistance had to be implemented without provoking the hordes of Communist Chinese to enter the fray and also to avoid resorting to nuclear escalation. With this delicate balance in mind, President Truman flew out to Wake Island (1951) to meet with General MacArthur to relieve him as Supreme Commander in Korea. President Truman believed that MacArthur was committed to launching a total invasion of North Korea that would take him into Manchuria; thereby, inciting a major conflict with China. The new era, however, dictated a policy of containment of aggressive adversaries rather than the achievement of total victory and unconditional surrender as was the case in WWII. It was later to be learned that the containment policy of Soviet aggression, as fathered by George F. Kennan, head of the State Department's first policy planning staff (1947-1950), was intended to be political and diplomatic rather than military. However, the subsequent reconfiguration of this policy under the "hawkish" advice of Paul Nitze, National Security Council under President Harry Truman, led to the military involvement in Korea and Vietnam to curb the "domino effect" of a Communist takeover.

As we entered the '50s the Soviet Union, our ally in WWII, was now being seen as a deadly adversary following the deliverance of nuclear secret documents by Ethel and Julius Rosenberg (1951) and the subsequent buildup of nuclear weapons under Stalin's sinister leadership. Children were taught to "duck and cover" in response to an attack by the Soviets. The Strategic Air Command carried on 24-hour operations in which heavy bombers loaded with nuclear weapons were constantly airborne in rotating shifts. There was also a frenetic buildup of land-based intercontinental ballistic missile sites and stealthy nuclear-armed submarines prowled the oceans on both sides. Then, in October of 1957 the Soviet Union launched Sputnik, the first satellite to orbit the earth and, as we heard the peculiar beep as it circled the globe, the country was shocked into an awareness of how deficient our schools had been in teaching math and science. Movies such as "On the Beach" and "Fail-Safe" dramatized the cataclysmic possibilities of a military miscalculation. The idea was that any attack would be met with devastating retaliation and so the policy was called "MAD" for Mutually Assured Destruction. Senator Joe McCarthy of Wisconsin was conducting "communists behind every bush" inquisitions in the U.S. Senate and many people in education, government and entertainment had their reputations ruined by association and innuendo. Following WWII Americans were said to see themselves as innocent and invincible—innocent in that we were on the side of righteousness and goodness and invincible in that we were heroic and unconquerable. This was demonstrated in the television shows of the 1950s. The country seemed to revel in the innocent and naive family life of Ozzie and Harriet, Father Knows Best, Leave It to Beaver and the most popular Happy Days, as well as the invincible American hero "westerns" such as, Gun Smoke, The Virginian and Rawhide. At the same time a new form of irrepressible music emerged–the rock beat. Chubby Checker, Elvis Presley, Jerry Lee Lewis, Little Richard and Buddy Holly, to name a few, were giving music a new sense of emotional expression and displacing the dreamy, sentimental ballads of the WWII years. The Beatles were forming a style of music in Liverpool that was going to ride the crest of a social revolution that would eventually see its zenith at the great Woodstock "happening" in Bethel, New York. "Beatniks" of the '50s were giving way to "Hippies" of the '60s. Jack Kerouac and Allen Ginsberg offered young people a kind of ragbag philosophy of rebellion and alienation from the established American culture. Joan Baez took us back to a purer and more distilled time in American life in the form of rarefied folk music and at the same time she and Ira Sandperl, her political mentor, established the Institute for the Study of Non-Violence in Carmel Valley, California in deference to the earlier Mahatma Gandhi movement in India.

As we entered the 1960s, there appeared to be a "Crossing of the Rubicon" of social change in the United States. In the major cities, particularly in San Francisco, drug experimentation and "free love" offered the illusion of creating a new world by "tuning in, turning on, and dropping out" as espoused by the drop-out Harvard Psychology Professor, Dr. Timothy Leary. At the same time a kind of psychological regression to earlier times in American history seemed to capture the imagination of the people. We lost ourselves in the folk music of Peter, Paul and Mary, the Weavers, Pete Seeger, Bob Dylan, and Arlo Guthrie—the son of Woody Guthrie. When we traded in the sensible conservatism of Dr. Benjamin Spock for the "spacey" liberalism of Dr. Timothy Leary, we began a long slide into diffusion of American culture as we knew it. A redress of the inequalities of the past among selective minority groups took on attitudes of hyper-atonement for specific historical ethnic transgressions. African-American militancy as espoused by Malcom X in the South and in the form of the Black Panthers in the West emerged under the leadership of Eldridge Cleaver and Angela Davis. Mario Savio shouted and stormed at Sather Gate and the U.C. Berkeley campus became a focal point for crusades against the educational and political establishments while an African-American woman in Montgomery, Alabama by the name of Rosa Parks refused to go to the back of the bus. What followed were increasingly intense confrontations between the African-American people and white authority figures. A young visionary preacher by the name of Martin Luther King, Jr. took a position at the head of a movement for equal rights and non-violent civil disobedience and prayed for people to be judged on the "content of their character rather than the color of their skin." In 1964, Civil Rights legislation seemed to promise a fruition of the "dreams" of MLK and the African-American people and, at the same time, would presage the foreboding of difficult times ahead. Unfortunately, instead of getting King's message, the African-American society began aligning itself in distinctly oppositional camps and referring to itself, divisively, as "Black" as opposed to "White." In March of 1991 a young African-American by the name of Rodney King was the subject of police brutality after a DUI stop and it happened to be caught on video by a bystander. The result was catastrophic. Resentments smoldered and then erupted in the devastating Watt riots of South-Central Los Angeles, almost tearing that city apart and Rodney King, himself, appealed for a cessation of violence in his pathetic statement, "Can't we just all get along." In all this confusion and divisive anger, Blacks (as they preferred to be called) were invested with inordinate and indulgent deference while ignoring the fact that most all immigrant groups that originally entered this country or even those indigenous to it were oppressed in some form.

In the Black populations of America there developed a bifurcated attitude toward American society. On the one hand there were those who looked upon their U.S. citizenship as an opportunity to strive and to become assimilated into American culture. They were to make contributions as responsible members of the society as others had done. At the same time there were those who chose to revel in their rage and feelings of victimization. The latter groups were to present a very difficult problem because their demonstrated attitude of belligerence and hostility was one of getting back and getting even for the sins of the past and the battle cry was "racism." Those who were to persist in this oppositional attitude seemed not to realize that their best interests lie in non-violent persuasion, as their great leader MLK had taught, rather than in attitudes of paranoid hostility. The enslavement and exploitation of the African Negro was a terrible thing; however, Negro slavery was not the only form of indentured servitude in this country. Consider the plight of the Chinese, many of whom were abducted and brought to this country to be used to build the railroads in the West and the Irish immigrants who built the railroads in the East suffered much the same indignities as the Negro—and don't forget the indigenous native American Indians who were so badly treated and demoralized that most now exist only in a state of helpless and depressed dependency. The Negro people were not the only ethnic group to suffer oppression and exploitation in America. It is true that no other ethnic group was brought to this country in chains and sold in a public square, but we must also remember that the greatest suffering this country had ever known occurred during our own Civil War (1861-1865) in its struggle to emancipate the African-Americans from the bonds of slavery and tyranny. The subsequent struggle of prejudicial intolerance and racism that was to follow was a moral issue and a legal one and should have been dealt with as such. Once it became the law of the land that the African-American was entitled to the same civil/legal considerations as the rest of the population, issues of prejudicial intolerance ought to have become a moral one and racism, as we have come to know it, ought never to have become a source of civil manipulation. It could be argued that legislating personal morality, social sensitivity and good manners is a pointless endeavor. Despite the unfairness, however, with which some ethnic groups were treated in this country, some of their own served brilliantly and courageously to defend the United States in time of war. Reference the Navajo Code Talkers of WWII who made important contributions to winning the war in the Pacific against the Japanese and the segregated Tuskegee Airmen (a group of African-American fighter pilots) who escorted bombers over Europe in a protective umbrella that was completely successful in fighting off enemy air attacks. Japanese-Americans who were imprisoned in isolation camps during WWII gave their sons to the Armed Forces who served magnificently in the struggle against the Nazi armies of Adolf Hitler and African American soldiers throughout American history stood tall with other ethnic groups in defense of freedom and the emancipation from slavery and the right to live as free men.

In my view, however, indulgent acquiescence toward the African-American and then Hispanic groups selectively beginning in the 1960s threatened the integrity of what this nation had always represented, i.e., a society of hard working and industrious individuals, by tradition, but also a society of well-defined cultural mores and idealistic values that we shared with each other as a New World culture in trust and community interests. This is not to say that African American and Hispanic groups were inherently incompetent to hold their own in America but they did have a need for effective assistance and encouragement in the form of education and training and the opportunity to succeed. They did not need to be warehoused and custodialized in "projects" or administered to as helpless wards as in the case of the American Indian. Our liberalized "Great Society" programs only indulged and disavowed those groups as a way of dismissing the problem and perhaps atoning for a national sense of guilt.

The Great Society intentions were highly ambitious in a "social engineering" sense. It was intended to address the injustices perpetrated against minority groups with reference to civil rights and it did, which was good, but it also led to injustices toward those who were not allowed to compete for jobs because of "affirmative action" policies. Discrimination went the other way. A white person, highly qualified, could not get a job as a counselor in a community college because those jobs were given first to a minority person, who might have been less qualified. This was because of the civil rights legislation that attempted to redress the discrimination of the past. The "war on poverty" provided aid to families with dependent children in the form of housing projects and money and food stamps but led to, what some believe, was a further destruction of the African-American family. It encouraged women to have more children to get more money and it encouraged men to shirk on their responsibilities to father and provide for their children. In the education area, many federal resources were channeled into helping the learning handicapped and preparing young ones in the form of "head start" programs but it seems that money was directed in such a way as not to be accounted for and that gave rise to abuses such that a school administrator would spend his allocation for the year on anything in order to not have his quota reduced for the following year. It also seemed to play into legislation to relieve homeowners of paying a fair share of taxes to support the schools. Health legislation benefited many but most were older people on Medicare and those below the poverty line with Medicaid. On the other hand, the middle-class working people began to suffer because of increasing costs of medical insurance. Consumer protection attempted to shore up deficiencies in business and industry but gave people a feeling of having a "big brother" always looking down on you. Government seemed to be everywhere and involved in our daily life. And, finally, there was the issue of the environment. The movement to preserve the environment was a good thing. We were hearing of polluted lakes and streams and waste dumps of hazardous material that threatened the lives of children, but here, again, it seemed as though there was an overzealousness that made it hard for loggers to cut down trees and regulate the forests.

In San Francisco, Enrico Banducci's "Hungry Eye" located at 546 Broadway Street was instrumental in starting the careers of Mort Sahl and Lenny Bruce, Ronnie Schell, Bill Cosby, the Kingston Trio, Vince

Guaraldi, Glen Yarborough, Professor Irwin Corey and the Mamas and the Pappas. It was "in" to take pot shots at the establishment and the "flower children" started gravitating to the corner of Haight and Ashbury. What began there as an innocent experimentation with LSD, marijuana and communal living under the pseudo-spiritual leadership of the drug gurus later became festooned with sickly flowers of hostility, disease and "bad trips." It was a time of blasphemous defiance and misguided dissent. President John Kennedy was reluctantly sending "technical advisers" (1961) to assist the "Westernized" Vietnamese in the south with their struggle against the military insurgence of the Communist Vietnamese in the north. Senator J. William Fulbright of Arkansas and Senator Wayne Morse of Oregon presided over the Senate Foreign Relations Committee and daily made appeals to common sense and the Constitutional errors of committing U.S. Armed Forces to that Southeast Asia civil war. They further tried to point out that our military involvement in Vietnam would be very weakly supported by SEATO, the Southeast Asia Treaty Organization, and even questioned the constitutionality of our involvement in that alliance. All this fell on deaf ears because of the din of hysteria and confusion about stemming the "domino effect" of Communist aggression. The whole Southeast Asia situation put Kennedy in a difficult bind because of his reluctance to fully engage U.S. troops in that emerging war. He had been burned by the "Bay of Pigs" fiasco in the early part of his administration and did not want to entertain any such future failures. In the 1960s, the Nation was in a state of extreme worry when it was learned in 1962 that the Soviets had installed long range missiles in Cuba that could reach vital areas in the U.S. The new President John F. Kennedy ordered Soviet Premier Nikita Khrushchev to take them out unless there be certain retaliation that would likely lead to a nuclear war. The whole world stood on the brink of global devastation. Fortunately, the matter was resolved when the U.S. agreed to withdraw its missile sites in Turkey and allowed Khrushchev to save face. A year later, in 1963, we were shocked and horrified by the assassination of President John F. Kennedy and, in 1968, a promising Presidential aspirant, Robert "Bobby" Kennedy and a charismatic leader of the Civil Rights Movement, Martin Luther King, Jr. were also assassinated.

In recent history the American culture has undergone a diffusion of what once were valued traditions. At the same time, attempts to redress the wrongs of past injustices took on cataclysmic sweeps of change. An excessive liberalization of laws and "Great Society" welfare programs provided special deference to those who would abuse the system or adapt to a further diminution of personal effectiveness and, at the same time, smolder with hostile/dependent resentment. Judicial systems and "due process of law" were indulgently administered to and even those who had been convicted of terrible crimes against humanity and were regarded still as invested with the same rights and privileges as the law-abiding citizen. Endless appeals and shortened sentences for "good behavior" gave the socio-pathically disposed tremendous manipulative advantages. In my view, excesses of the American Civil Liberties Union provided criminals in court with rights far beyond equal fairness with an offended plaintiff and prison confinement became couched with television, telephones, workout facilities, conjugal visits, weekend passes and higher education in the Law. In some cases, even those who were incarcerated received Social Security payments under Supplemental Security Income (SSI). Criminal justice began taking precedence over citizen justice.

Radical and poorly constructed legislation was impulsively implemented to make things right and equal for those who were thought to be the most oppressed. Instead of upgrading the quality of schools in the impoverished areas with a plan of gradual and consistent improvement, Judge W. Arthur Garrity Jr. of the United States District Court for the District of Massachusetts, mandated that children from "good" neighborhood schools spend wasted hours on buses while being transported to "bad" schools across town. Instead of a well thought out plan of education and training for impoverished minority groups, we launched an indulgent welfare program that only served to further incapacitate and demoralize people. This only served to breed dependency and resentment in too many under-privileged Americans who could have been better served in more productive ways. Instead, we spotted African-American, Hispanic and American Indians with "affirmative action" advantages, further lowering standards of achievement and productivity while at the same time surreptitiously labeling them as inferior and incompetent. Tokenism and mediocrity were the standards of those years. Some benefited, true, but we understand now that most did not.

Anger, resentment and dependency set the stage for a massive avoidance reaction with devastating flights from reality into a drug culture which had, in turn, unleashed the greatest social disorder this Nation has ever known as a new kind of violent crime was emerging on the American scene. Horrendous, irrational and incomprehensible assaults, even toward children, began occurring with regularity. Military assault firearms with rapid fire capability that were designed for war were being bought up and used regularly by dangerous individuals with criminal records because there was no effective control over these weapons. The National Rifle Association wielded tremendous power with their lobby in Congress and legislators backed off from taking responsible action. During this time there was an excessive liberalizing bias toward justice for criminal behavior and the California Supreme Court virtually allowed repeat violent offenders to walk the streets and continue to practice their monstrous profession—and the rest of the nation followed that insidious lead. We had not learned as a society that some twisted individuals commit their horrible crimes "so they can relieve tension, feel pleasure and get a good night's sleep," as one inmate put it. This kind of indulgent "liberal" thinking was to also devalue the quality of education for young people because it became the right of errant and incorrigible children to remain mainstreamed in the classroom. Teachers had to spend much of their valuable teaching time controlling those who would not cooperate. The threat of litigation hung in the air like a bad smell and accountability in the form of increased bureaucratic paperwork further interfered with teacher effectiveness. In my experience, I discovered that school administrators found justification for increasing their ranks and their salaries. The teacher, who was the real professional, caught the backwater sludge and frustration that comes from a diminished status and impossible expectations. As classroom populations increased, beyond the point for effective teaching, school funding started a progressive decline so that the younger, more enthusiastic and better trained who were the last hired might have to sweat out whether or not their contract would be renewed for the following year–even before they ever had a chance to make their contributions. The older and less effective were protected by tenure.

During this time it became clear that disengagement from the Vietnam War was imperative. Our involvement had virtually torn this country apart and had come close to creating civil anarchy. In 1968, the Democratic

Convention in Chicago had produced scenes reminiscent of Nazi Germany prior to the advent of WWII. After the election of Richard Nixon in 1969, President Nixon and Dr. Henry Kissinger, Secretary of State, had secretly orchestrated the bombing of Cambodia creating further unrest and dissent among the American people. That same year Neil Armstrong, the first man on the moon, saluted the world with, "One small step for a man, one giant step for mankind." The anti-war movement under the leadership of Jerry Rubin, the organizer of the VDC (Vietnam Day Committee) and Abby Hoffman, (and the Chicago 7) played important roles in the disruption of the 1968 Democratic National Convention in Chicago. Then in 1971, Daniel Ellsberg, Pentagon military analyst during the 60s, released the Pentagon Papers to the New York Times, which the Nixon administration attempted to bar from publication by court order. Then on June 29, 1971, U.S. Senator Mike Gavel of Alaska entered 4,100 pages of the Pentagon Papers into the record of his subcommittee. This allowed the press and the public to see the real picture of what was occurring in Vietnam. All of these events, as well as the break-in of Richard Nixon's collaborators into the Democratic Party Headquarters at the Watergate Hotel, exerted enough pressure on him to disgracefully resign from the Presidency. Then came the "honorable" withdrawal of American forces in Vietnam in 1975 but in reality, it was a humiliating defeat. We all saw on television the frantic scrambling for passage on helicopters atop the U.S. Embassy building as the United States Armed

Forces evacuated Saigon. The degree of discord in this country over the Vietnam War had been horribly punctuated at Kent State University when students were fired upon by members of the Ohio State National Guard back in 1970 during a peaceful demonstration. We later learned that General Westmoreland and his commanders had falsified reports as to the status of the war so President Johnson could entertain a false sense of impending victory. It was later learned that Robert S. McNamara, the Secretary of Defense and the recognized architect of the Vietnam War, later admitted that going into Vietnam was a colossal mistake. And so, for the first time in U.S. history, a president was forced to resign in disgrace (1974) for obstructing justice involving a common burglary. And all the while, as we entered the early 1970s, we were laughing at the preposterous Bunker family that lived on Houser Street that put into comic relief some of the important social issues of the day.

In June of 1978, the Jarvis-Gann Proposition 13 further eroded the financial support for the California public schools, which in the 1960s had been ranked nationally as among the best but had fallen to 48th in many surveys of student achievement. Some had disputed Proposition 13 's direct role in the move to State financing of public schools because schools financed mostly by property taxes were declared unconstitutional in Serrano vs. Priest and Proposition 13 was then passed, partially as a result of that case. California's spending per pupil was the same as the national average until about 1985, when it began dropping, which led to another referendum. Proposition 98 required a certain percentage of the State's budget to be directed towards education. It could be argued that all citizens of California and, indeed, the whole United States have a vested interest in educating its young and property taxes should be proportionately assessed to all land and property owners. It seems that the primary argument for the "People's Initiative to Limit Property Taxes" was that older Californians should not be priced out of their homes through high taxes. This could have been remedied by allowing a special exemption as they do in some States for the elderly and those living on modest incomes.

Even juvenile probation officers who had some leverage in the past to intercede with the incorrigible individuals lost that capacity due to the excessive liberalization of Juvenile Court Laws passed in California in 1961. Children were entitled to be represented in Juvenile Court by their own attorney—very often in opposition to those of their own parents. Civil rights became such a priority issue that even the mentally incompetent were released from institutional care, under the leadership of Governor Ronald Reagan (1967-1975), and put out on the streets to fend for themselves, giving rise to a homeless phenomenon never before seen in this country. The reluctance to address the problems forthrightly among our legislators, judges and parole boards had paved the way for unspeakable atrocities committed by violent felons who were freed to prowl the communities of law-abiding citizens and devastate their lives. The "new liberalism" had reduced government to a farcical drama without the will to assert itself in the interest of the common good. It had instigated rage among majorities and minorities as well. It bred a generation of poorly educated, poorly parented and poorly inspired subcultures who would seek to waste their lives in hopelessness and drug addiction or to vent their rage and resentment in violent acts of vengeance and terrorism. Furthermore, the emergence of social discord and resentment had seduced the legal profession in a way that subverts its integrity. Though the practice of law as a profession is inherently a noble social enterprise that seeks to ensure a sense of justice and fairness within the society, it has also attracted individuals with less noble character who, in the guise of nobility, have created further problems by generating excessive and greed-inspired litigation. Because of excessive litigation, the medical profession felt compelled to practice what is called "defensive" medicine, which involved many procedures that were really unnecessary and very expensive. Likewise, there was also a reluctance of pharmaceutical companies to provide the new innovations of science and technology because they could be sued for enormous amounts of money if one of their products caused someone harm. The focus was not on the massive benefit, but on the harm that might occur to a very few. From a social point of view it did appear that over the past 50 years there has been a diminution of community feeling and trust among the people and a loss of confidence in government systems and government officials, themselves, have become discouraged and disheartened. No longer can agreements be honored by a shake of hands as was the custom in the United States for generations. Some of our best legislators have left government because they feel constantly frustrated to get important things done and because the old comradeship of the Congress has been replaced by hostile partisanship and self-interest.

One of our most honored institutions, the U.S. Mail Service, which for generations had been a respected and dependable function of government, has become inordinately expensive and often subject to poor morale. In past years, those who delivered the mail were held in high esteem for their responsibility and service because every piece and letter was known to be important to the receiver but now it is so encumbered with "junk" and cheap advertising that its value has been diminished—while the price of a stamp keeps going up.

Women began asserting themselves and opting for equality with men in business and government. The concept of the "super mom" found a place in American jargon. Betty Friedan and Gloria Steinem led the Feminist movement and NOW (National Organization for Women) took extreme positions about the newly emerging role of women in America. Some advocated a complete independence from the domination of men, escaping the yoke of submissiveness and docility and engaging the world of men on an equal basis. The new movement made stay-at-home mothers feel intimidated and diminished while others, like Phyllis Shlafley, espoused the more traditional activities of women such as motherhood, homemaking and building character in their children while remaining the queen of the household. This revolution among American women seemed to confuse and threaten men who were emotionally unequipped to deal with such changes. Men began to search for solutions in all-male sensitivity groups in order to understand the changing roles of women and to what extent they could assert themselves in this new context. As men became more sensitized toward women, women became more frustrated toward men. It became a very confusing arena of gender functions. This led to extreme reactions on both sides and laid the groundwork for such mating doctors as John Gray and his "Men Are from Mars, Women Are from Venus" books to lend some clarity to the issue and the whole nation teetered on the horns of this dilemma.

During the early '70s, about the time of Nixon's resignation in disgrace, OPEC (The Organization of Petroleum Exporting Countries) had decided to put the squeeze on the American oil industry by raising the price of their products (1973) and causing unbelievable gas lines on the streets of America. Petroleum intensive areas in the U.S. like Houston went into a severe economic depression and many had to leave the area and look for work elsewhere.

On Sept. 17, 1978, a meeting was held at Camp David attended by Egyptian President Anwar Sadat, Israeli Prime Minister Menachem Begin and U.S. President Jimmy Carter as an attempt to bring peace between Israel and Egypt following several military confrontations. A peace treaty was signed on March 26, 1979. In the Middle East, the good will initiative of Anwar Sadat of Egypt led to the Camp David Accords and set the stage for the remarkable developments toward peaceful coexistence between the Israeli and Arab factions–an ardent hope that, unfortunately, was never realized.

In 1982, there began a softening of relations between the Soviet Union and the United States following a letter to the Premier, Andropov, written by a ten-year-old girl from Manchester, Maine by the name of Samantha Smith. She politely inquired if there could be some way that she and her friends could grow up without the worry of a nuclear war. Because of her innocent and sincere letter she was invited to spend two weeks in the Soviet Union among the children of that country. In a sense, she was the first female goodwill ambassador to the Soviet Union. This was the first softening of U.S./Soviet relations since WWII. Following this event Gorbachev, who had been Andropov's protégé, assumed leadership when Andropov died and that was the beginning of the end of the Communist Soviet Union as we knew it.

By the end of the 1970s and into the '80s, people became more sensitized to the vulnerability of human life and it was during this time that a consciousness spread across the land having to do with safety, environmental protection and life affirming health concerns. There were movements to clean up polluted lakes and rivers, toxic waste dumps, putting seat belts in automobiles and making cars more survivable and paying attention to diet and exercise. Medical miracles were beginning to happen frequently. In foreign lands, Amnesty International and the concept of human rights became a significant movement and at home Greenpeace and The Sierra Club gave us a new appreciation of whales, dolphins and all living creatures (and trees) great and small and at the same time a mysterious new virus among the homosexual community began making an appearance.

In 1979, our Embassy personnel were suddenly taken hostage in Iran following the defection of the U.S. supported Shah and the return of the Ayatollah Khomeini.

Foreign policy had failed again. Interest rates skyrocketed, further crippling the economy and public confidence. On the day of Ronald Reagan's swearing-in ceremony (1980) to the Presidency, the hostages in Iran were released. It was later discovered that this came as a result of a clandestine arms deal carried out by undetermined agents and allowed Reagan "plausible denial" of any awareness of the matter. Later an ambitious Marine Lt. Colonel by the name of Oliver North would appear prominently in other clandestine activities surrounding the Iran- Contra affair. The CIA was also found to be perpetrating sinister plots to overthrow the Sandinistas in Nicaragua. Communism was being cultivated in Central America and that was not tolerable except, of course, in Cuba. We had been burned there as a result of the Bay of Pigs fiasco during the Kennedy administration and after the Cuban missile crisis we decided that we had better peacefully coexist with Fidel Castro, hoping that with some mild embargoes his own people would bring him down. Getting back to Reagan, the super optimist, super communicator, whose denial of the "deep pocket" tendencies of avaricious people and his supply side economics enabled opportunistic entrepreneurs to pad their pockets with over-extended government funding. Many short-term jobs were created erecting office space that was never used. At the cost of government solvency, over-extended credit provided enormous closing profits for the wheelers and dealers that probably set the stage for the hardships and "downsizing" of the '90s. In later years plant closings, hostile mergers and layoffs came to be commonplace events. As a result of the excesses of the '80s and the fiscal irresponsibility of the Executive and Congressional oversight committees who looked the other way along with Reagan's tax cuts and crash arms race spending, to break the back of the Soviets we became the greatest debtor nation in the world whereas we had once been the greatest creditor nation on Earth. For some people it was a time to make hay and jump on the band-wagon of excess while plunging the nation into colossal debt and, at the same time, collapsing the old reliable Savings and Loan industry to the tune of $260 billion.

It is true that this country enjoyed some years of prosperity and high morale. Interest rates and inflation came down under Reagan's leadership, but a failure of governmental integrity and financial responsibility culminated in the loss of the lives of American astronauts and a beloved teacher in the disaster of the Challenger space shuttle when the urgency to launch under very adverse conditions and for political aggrandizement resulted in a catastrophic failure for want of an "O" ring.

The enormous nuclear arms race and "wild west" showdown with the Soviets did appear to break the back of the already disintegrating communist system. Reagan's single-mindedness of purpose in helping to defeat the "Evil Empire" will probably go down in history as his greatest contribution; although, the eight years of "Reaganomics" had tripled the national debt from $900 billion when he took office to more than $2.8 trillion at the end of his term. All the while HIV infection became a frightening obsession because every day we learned of the skyrocketing escalation of this mysterious and fatal disease. While the AIDS epidemic began to jump to alarming proportions, excessive liberal persuasions provoked among homosexuals a wild and hysterical emergence from "the closet" and, at the same time, promoted, aggressively, a normalization and justification of the lifestyle to the public at large—and the AIDS epidemic rolled on. It became clear just how devastating this disease really was and never again would the word "gay" have the innocent and happy meaning as before. Even children now had to be introduced to the sordid facts of this terrible disease and its transmission. Childhood could no longer be a time of innocence and carefree exploration. It now became a time of wariness, hypervigilance and premature prurient knowledge. Tragic stories of innocent children being afflicted by contaminated blood supplies were beginning to headline the news and some were advocating a testing of the entire population and a sequestration of those who had been found to be infected.

It was during the closing years of the 1980s that President George Herbert Walker Bush and his advisers gravely miscalculated the will and intentions of Saddam of Iraq that, in turn, led to the very destructive and costly "Desert Storm." During the Clinton administration that followed, the timidity and indecisiveness in the White House allowed for the butchery and mayhem to continue in Bosnia, Serbia, and Croatia from 1992 to 1995. And when the Clinton administration took over in 1992, complex divisions of interests emerged which further accentuated the political differences between a liberal Chief Executive and a conservative Congress, however, instead of resolving problems and making purposeful legislation we got "gridlock" and mean-spirited antagonism. Issues that required the goodwill of the Congress as well as the Executive branch ranged from job creation and security, declining wages for workers (while enormous raises occurred in industry executive salaries and bonuses), minimum wage issues, the role of gays and women in the military, universal and portable health insurance, Medicare, Medicaid and Social Security, the moral questions surrounding abortion, "workfare," funding and standards for education, and what to do about crime and drugs, and don't forget gun control. We had become, by far, the most violent nation in the world and guns were the weapon of choice. Other more technical/political issues emerged as to the line-item veto, PAC campaign funding and the power of lobbyists in government, the feasibility of a third party, taxation unfairness and complexity, term limits, balancing the budget, reducing the size of the bloated federal government and returning more power to the States to solve their own social and economic problems and, not least, ethics. Since Watergate, the government seemed to have turned inward upon itself to present at least outwardly an image of self-purgation and impeccable morality; that is, until President Clinton's impeachment for sexual indiscretions in the Oval Office of the White House with Monica Lewinsky. Before he left the White House in 2001, President Clinton pardoned 100 plus convicted felons whose offenses (U.S. Dept. of Justice) ranged from conspiracy to drug trafficking, to tax evasion, to aiding and abetting, to forgery and perjury. It was alarming that a president could get away with perjury, an indiscriminate pardoning of criminals and setting of much more lenient standards for young people as to just what constitutes sexual behavior.

The great economic issues of the '90s came to be known as NAFTA and GAT (The North American Free Trade Agreement and the General Agreement on Trade) which some fear would further erode the standards of quality and excellence that had once been proudly shown on the label "Made in the U.S.A," Ross Perot had given convincing arguments to the effect that passage of these agreements would cause a "great sucking sound" as many of our industries would rush to other countries where cheap labor was abundant further depleting our own labor force and standard of living. Cheaply produced commodities would flood the American market and cause American economic values to further decline. Our aggravating trade deficit with Japan in autos had embarrassed our own auto industry because they had let quality deteriorate and costs rise to where Americans buying more Japanese vehicles. They were simply better. That kind of competition was healthy because it would motivate the American auto industry to wake up and produce a better product–but it didn't. Our big industries were entrenched in their belief that nothing could effectively compete with American productivity. It would take a virtual collapse of the U.S. auto industry in 2008 and a bail out of enormous government funds to make major re-adjustments in how American industry viewed its true place in the economic realities of the 21 st century. Most would agree that it is not in the interests of the United States to isolate itself from the rest of the world; however, it must enter into world trade agreements with some control and moderation. The U.S. ought not allow the standards of a third world nation to uncontrollably subvert those of our own country and yet we must be aware that there are emerging nations such as China and India who are becoming more competitive due to increased focus on education and a workforce that will work for cheaper wages.

As an explanation for all the unrest and disturbances in this society, many blame our violent culture, others our lack of religious training and taking religion out of the schools, others lament poor parenting and still others, political corruption and unworthy role models for the young. After all, we do see evidence of all this deterioration daily in our news broadcasts. We see children shooting other children in their classrooms and even crazed adults doing the same. In 1995 we all saw O.J. Simpson having been acquitted of murdering his wife, Nicole Brown Simpson, and her friend, Ronald Goldman, and then the cameras trained in on "White" and "Black" reactions to the verdict. The "Whites" couldn't believe it and the "Black" law students in

Atlanta were overjoyed–testifying again to the continued bitterness and dissension within the black/white issue.

We see squabbles over whether or not to allow a judge to place the Ten Commandments in his courtroom. Parents seem desperate for answers to questions about how to raise their children and television shows attempt to bring on professionals of one stripe or another to answer such questions. It seems as our technology advances, our social maturity is falling behind. We see violence and poor sportsmanship in our high schools, our professional arenas and even in parent supervised organized sports events for children. At the same time, ball players and entertainers are rewarded with enormous amounts of money while teachers and those whose responsibility it is to build a foundation for the future of this society in its youth are barely rewarded with a living wage.

We would do well to reconsider the moral and ethical ideals that our forefathers diligently provided for us. They were based on the best of acquired knowledge and wisdom of western civilization. We have been ignoring, it seems, the pearls of our heritage and instead have been groveling in the domain of our lower natures. Instead of turning toward those baser forces and boldly confronting them, we have been turning away in the service of unrestrained accommodation and allowing the vulnerable young people of our society to become overwhelmed by the poison.

William Pollack, Ph.D., in his book, "Real Boys" suggested that those who are the most vulnerable will break down first. It is analogous to being susceptible to asthma and living in a polluted air environment. Dr. Pollack went on to say that in our society boys are trained to establish a "mask of masculinity" and so repress their tender or "feminine" feelings. Boys, therefore, cannot express sadness, loneliness or feelings of alienation without suffering ridicule from their peers and even from their parents in many cases. Only anger and aggressiveness are acceptable.

So, in the pall and confusion of disjointed purposes our government has been crippled and unable to resist the pressures of self-interest groups and "victimized" minorities. We have become so fragmented in consensual purposes that we have become a society ruled by the self-centered goals of special interest groups rather than "the rule of the majority" as was originally intended. Crisis reactions replaced long term and thoughtful planning. In my view, in trying to please everyone, the government has become an unwieldy, over-fed, effete organism and the nation has become burdened with social disorder, cultural diffusion, colossal debt and undisciplined spending.

As the new millennium approached, people were afraid that computers that had not been programmed properly would cause chaos and total disruption of financial transactions throughout the world. Fortunately, this did not happen and that anxiety was put to rest. Instead, as the new Bush administration took over the reins of government, the country was hit with a catastrophic event unseen since Pearl Harbor in 1941. On September 11th of 2001, a hi-jacking of four American airliners by Islamic radical terrorists crashed into the World Trade Center and the Pentagon and flight 93 was heroically prevented from its intended target in Washington, DC by a few Americans who were unwilling to be commandeered by a few demented terrorists.

Approximately 3,000 people were brutally and senselessly killed that day. In response to this tragedy, the Bush administration set out to exact justice in retaliation by dishonestly contriving a justification to attack Iraq on the alleged determination that Saddam Hussein was stock piling nuclear weapons to be used against the U.S. It was later determined that there was no truth in this assumption. The inner circle of George W. Bush, Dick Cheney, Donald Rumsfeld and David Addington executed a war with Iraq with no pre-planning or circumspection as to how an occupation might be accomplished effectively. As it turned out there was an insurgency uprising that would cost the lives of thousands of American soldiers and Iraqi civilians and set the stage for horrible episodes of torture.

For the next several years there was to be gross mismanagement of the occupation and a build-up of ill will against the U.S. throughout the world—and a loss of trust and faith in our own leadership and national purpose. Meanwhile, we became more embroiled in the Afghanistan situation and this opened up another war. The very sad thing that happened during this time was that the "No Child Left Behind" bill that was espoused by Bush during his early years in the White House was not financed as was intended in order for the Bush administration to finance the war in Iraq and Afghanistan—a congressional effort that would have had positive impact on the children of this country was sacrificed for Bush's unconstitutional war in the Middle East. The American people were once again told lies in order to justify an "unjust war" costing billions of dollars and a great number of American and Iraqi lives—and a consequent further decline in America's stature and moral leadership throughout the world.

George W. Bush was re-elected for second term over John Kerry of Massachusetts and New Orleans was hit with Katrina, a devastating and costly storm with great loss of human life and property. This all occurred because the banks and levees that protected the lower parishes were known to be incapable of withstanding excessively high winds and tides. Nothing was done about it by the Corp of Engineers who complained that they were simply not provided with sufficient federal funds to do the work. Before and, after the devastation, the Bush administration proved to be unresponsive and ineffective in providing relief services. Where was the "compassionate conservatism" when it was needed?

Many abuses of corporate management began to emerge and the real estate market began feeling the effects of Greenspan's warning years ago about "irrational exuberance" and razzle-dazzle subprime mortgage loans and "creative financing" that allowed people to buy expensive homes as a speculation that the property would greatly increase in value and then could be either re-financed (with anticipated equity) or sold at a great profit. In the '80s and '90s, Wall Street came under the influence of a derivative debauchery of essentially "betting" on the market with greater and greater stakes. A warning was issued by Brooksley Born, chairperson of the Commodity Futures Trading Commission (the federal agency that oversees the futures and commodity options markets of derivative abuses), of a consequent severe downturn in the economy but her warnings were ignored. During her tenure on the CFTC, born lobbied congress and President Clinton to give the CFTC oversight of off-exchange markets for derivatives in addition to its role with respect to exchange-traded derivatives. Her warnings were opposed by Federal Reserve Chairman, Alan Greenspan, along with Robert Rubin and Lawrence Summers, whose economic philosophy followed that of Ronald Reagan and Ayn Rand in that "stay out of market regulation" and let the market regulate itself. It seemed that the country had been taken in by a pervasive sense of "getting it now" because for the present it seemed that America, as well as the world economy, was doing well. In recent times Greenspan has admitted he was wrong in his economic world view and a recent ruling by the Supreme Court (in striking down corporate campaign spending limits) has again opened the way for further abuses of the system and Brooksley Born is warning us again of further downturns in the market until we learn from our experience.

In his book, "Free Lunch," David Johnston reminds us of some important issues pertaining to our economic life in America:

"The power monger is no different from that of a cancer cell, which mindlessly seeks growth for the sake of its own self-interest until it overwhelms its host.

After WWII, our elected leaders worked to build and strengthen the middle class by investing in the brains of people, financing higher education through the GI bill, investing in science, education, public health and medical research and infrastructures.

In recent times we have turned away from these policies and government lobbying and special interests have allowed the gross and greedy to impose their will over the middle class and those least able to bear the burden thus subverting the foundations of this country.

Other countries refer to their health systems as "health service" rather than "health insurance" as it is in this country. We do use a business model instead of a service model."

Adam Smith tells us, "What improves the circumstances of the greater part can never be regarded as an inconvenience to the whole. No society can surely be flourishing and happy, of which the far greater part of the members is poor and miserable." America ranks 36th among nations in its rate of infant mortality in 2006.

President Bush said during the third election debate in 2004 that most of the tax cuts he sponsored went to low and middle-income Americans. That was not even close to the truth. In fact, most of the savings–53%–went to people with incomes in the top 10% over the first 15 years of the cuts, which began in 2001 and would have to be reauthorized to keep them in effect through 2015. More than 15% of the tax cuts went to the top tenth of 1%, a group that is over 300,000 people.

During Clinton's two terms he gave the richest of the super-rich a much bigger tax cut than even Bush. Under Clinton, their effective tax rate fell by almost eight cents on the dollar, under Bush it fell only five.

In terms of comparison with a list of 20 modern countries, the US ranks right below Portugal.

We now have almost three decades of experience with the idea that markets will solve our problems and the promises are not there. Many hundreds of billions of dollars have been diverted to the rich, leaving our schools, parks, and local government services starved for funds.

We pour billions into subsidies for sports teams and golf courses, a folly Adam Smith railed against in his day. Our health care system cost us far more than that of any other industrial country and yet we live shorter lives than Canadians, Europeans and the Japanese.

As the 2008 election year came upon us there was a strong feeling, it seems, among the people that we, as a nation, were heading in the wrong direction and real change was needed in order to set the Ship of State back on the right course. Ethics, morality and trust in our society and government had been eroding for many years.

We were sliding into what appeared to be a major recession or perhaps depression. Jobs began to disappear, unemployment started to rise to highs not seen since the early '30s and the U.S. auto industry started to hover on the edge of bankruptcy. The Arab-Israeli conflict continued to threaten the peace of the Middle East, and Iran posed a threat of developing a nuclear capability that would further destabilize the area. Pakistan, a nuclear power, presented itself as an unstable government and North Korea, again, appeared to be rattling its sabers. Amidst all this the American people elected a young man of African-American-Moslem descent, who campaigned on "change" and was so elected. He was a former president of the Harvard Law Review and a man of vision, leadership and a will to restore America to its intended destiny.

After electing a "change" president, many Americans appear to be regretting the changes being implemented by the new president and want change at a much slower pace. Many are now espousing the need to move slowly because it does seem that when too many changes are made too rapidly and extreme movement is made in any direction there will be an opposing reaction–it seems to be a law of nature. The great philosophers taught moderation. Too much too soon of anything can lead to trouble and take us to places where "even angels fear to tread." This seems to be the major discontent with the current Obama administration along with what is perceived as a conciliatory foreign policy. It is interesting to note here that the Obama administration has done far more than the previous Bush administration to eliminate the Al Qaeda threat.

However, our Ship of State has been far off course according to most and moving it back on course would have to entail a lot of discomfort and upheaval. It is questionable whether or not slow incremental degree changes will result in enough credible movement to provide a stimulus for further changes— our congress having much the disposition to deadlock itself in oppositional, contentious and partisan interests. Those politicians who have managed to ensconce themselves in their positions for many years seem to develop an investment to continue forming a web of personally advantageous networks. Knowing one's way around the "loop," so to speak, has its advantages but so can defeat the purpose of good and responsible government. Perhaps if term limits for Congressmen and Senators could be reestablished, as it is for the presidency, the return to the concept of the "citizen public servant" would help the elected officials to stop basing their legislative choices on catering to the will of their well healed constituency for campaign money and truly consider the common good of the country as a whole. Furthermore, the influence of lobbying in the legislature in order to influence the special interests of those with persuasive financial power, tends to defeat the interests of the "common good." Much needs to be done to restore the government to the will of the people rather than the will of a few. At the writing of this 2012 revision, it is the general consensus of the American people that our country is in a very dire situation with an enormous national debt that is rising beyond the capacity or will of our political leaders to control it, our very poor fiscal and monetary policies, the plunging real estate market and very high unemployment. In addition, there does appear to be an over-bloating of personnel employed in the government sector and that needs to be trimmed down considerably.

There is also the impending threat that large corporations will not hire as before because much of what is produced can be done robotically and those jobs that will be available in the future will require a high degree of technical training and education, which our educational system is failing to accommodate. This country is becoming less competitive in these areas than China and India. It does, therefore, seem to suggest that a great focus must be put upon the sector of our economy that deals with small businesses and start up enterprises and improved education along with substantial preventative medical care for all because a healthy society is more apt to be a contributing and productive society.

In a recent book published in 2011, the authors Weidemer, Weidemer and Spitzer have written about what they describe as the "multibubble" economy that is threatening to collapse our economy and send the world into a massive economic "correction" that will create severe hardships. They are warning that we must be prepared because this is determined to happen. So, what is a bubble economy? According to the aforementioned authors, "An economy that grows in a virtual upward spiral of multiple rising bubbles (real estate, stocks, private debt, dollar, and government debt) that interact to drive each other up, and that will inevitably fall in a vicious downward spiral as each falling bubble puts downward pressure on the rest, eventually pulling the whole economy down."

It does appear that greed and duplicity have become national virtues as competitive motivators for those at the top of the corporate and financial institutions ladder by "creating" incentives for the lower income populace to spend beyond their means.

At the time of the 2016 election the United States seems to have succumbed to the avaricious narcissistic inclinations of the times by putting into the sacrosanct office of the Presidency of the U.S. a highly successful but highly unethical businessman by the name of Donld J. Trump. Most Americans were willing to put aside the traditional values of the Nation for the sake of allegedly enhancing the economy. His campaign slogan, "Make America Great Again" or MAGA, seems to have captured the imagination of a particular group of people that bound them to the illusory siren call of Donald J. Trump.

When it became evident that the now President Trump made numerous promises to lower taxes and support the working middle class, his 10 campaign promises were as follows:

- He said he would build a wall and make Mexico pay for it.
- Temporarily ban Muslims from entering the U.S.
- Bring manufacturing jobs back saying, "I'm going to be the greatest job president, God ever created."

- Impose tariffs on goods made in China and Mexico.
- Renegotiate or withdraw from NAFTA and free-trade agreements and trans pacific partnerships.
- Fully repeal Obama care and replace it with a market-based alternative.
- Renegotiate the Iran deal.
- Leave social security as is.
- Cut taxes.
- Bomb and/or take the oil from ISIS.

According to FactCheck.ORG Trump's presidential record indicates that:

- The economy lost 2,876,000 jobs.
- The unemployment rate went up 6.3%
- Job Openings went up 25.7%
- Real Weekly Earnings went up 8.7%
- Economic Growth Rate went down 3.4%
- S&P went up 67.8%
- Median Household income went up 6%
- Poverty Rate went down 1.3%
- Murder rate went up 1.1%
- US-Mexico Border Apprehensions went up 14.7%
- Home Prices went up 27.5%
- Home Ownership up 2.1 points
- Corporate Profits went up 8.5%
- Federal Regulatory Restrictions went up 0.9%
- People Without Health Insurance rose to 3 million (NHIS)

- Food Stamp Recipients went down by 1.7%
- Coal Mining Jobs went down by 8,500
- Manufacturing Jobs went down by 154,000
- Federal Debt held by the Public went up by 50%
- Carbon Dioxide Emissions went down by 11.5%
- Trade deficit went up by 40%
- Consumer Price Index went up to 7.6%
- Handgun Production went up by 12.5%
- U.S. Crude Oil Production went up by 27.6%

Since Trump lost his bid for a second term in 2020 to the Democrat, Joe Biden, he adamantly refused to admit his defeat and insisted that the election was stolen from him by deceitful falsification of the election system. The whole matter was subjected to judicial scrutiny and found that the 2020 general election was in no way criminally tampered with or compromised—and to this day Trump still maintains that he is the rightful president of the U.S. Even though he is currently under indictment for 91 criminal offenses in several jurisdictions he is running again for the Presidency against the current President Joe Biden and, at this time, (April 18, 2024) he is being adjudicated in a New York Federal Court for felony offenses involving an illegal cover-up payoff of 130,000 for prostitution services with porn film star Stormy Daniels.

Because of his unsavory and self-serving personality and disregard for the conventional amenities such as gracefully yielding the office of the Presidency when a new President has been elected, he is considered disqualified to hold such an honorable position of leadership, however, many of his followers will say that they do not like him as a person but they admire his demonstrated boldness, business capabilities and his ability to get things done. He does exhibit the characteristics of a dictator, for which he seems to subscribe. His attitude in his business dealings do appear to be dictatorial and that trait has carried through in his Presidential office.

In addition to his current legal problems, he has been indicted for instigating and promoting an overthrow of our Constitutional government on Jan.6, 2021 with a mob that attacked and invaded the Capitol building while the Congress was in session legitimizing and confirming the official voting of the people for their choice of President. He is also indicted on "racketeering conspiracy" charges along with his 18 allies in meddling with the election.

Another indictment is the 37 accusations related to obstruction of justice as to the handling of classified documents which he refused to return to the proper authorities for 1 year claiming he was entitled to the documents as President.

Trump continues to maintain that he is completely innocent of all these allegations and charges and claims no responsibility for committing any crimes and that all these accusations and indictments he is completely innocent and he is being attacked by his political adversaries. Furthermore, if he is convicted of any of these crimes and denied the Presidency as he feels he deserves, he says, "It's going to be a bloodbath."

The U.S. has gone through trying times before but not as a Constitutional crisis and challenge to our essential way of life from the inside. One might argue about the Civil War of 1861 to 1865 but we must remember that this conflict was for the South to secede from the Union all-together to maintain their agricultural economy by means of slavery. The choice the American people must make is a choice between maintaining the Constitutional form of democratic, people driven government or an autocratic-dictatorial form as was characteristic of antiquity.

Part II

The Folly of the Criminal Justice System in America

According to reports of 2005 the National Institute of Justice found that the 5-year recidivism rate in America was 76.6% and the 3 years recidivism rate was 67.8%. The question is: what are we doing wrong as a society that so many of those who have been incarcerated for crimes are back in the prison system instead of living productive and "corrected" lives? This is a complex question that deserves a serious look since there is so much loss of human resources, potential and national wealth by not addressing the problem and seeking a better understanding of what moves a child toward anti-social attitudes and a life of criminality.

On April 22, 2014 The Bureau of Justice Statistics released: Recidivism of Prisoners in 30 States—Patterns from 2005 to 2010- Update. It reported the following:

About two-thirds (67.8%) of released prisoners were arrested for a new crime within 3 years, and three-quarters (76.6%) were arrested within 5 years.

Within 5 years of release, 82.1% of property offenders were arrested for a new crime, compared to 76.9% of drug offenders, 73.6% of public order offenders, and 71.3% of violent offenders.

More than a third (36.8%) of all prisoners who were arrested within 5 years of release were arrested within the first 6 months after release, with more than half (56.7%) arrested by the end of the first year.

Two in five (42.5%) released prisoners were either not arrested or arrested once in the 5 years after their release.

A sixth (16.1%) of released prisoners were responsible for almost half (48.4%) of the nearly 1.2 million arrests that occurred in the 5year follow-up period.

An estimated 10,9% of released prisoners were arrested in a state other than the one that released them during the 5-year follow-up period.

Within 5 years of release, 84.1% of inmates who were age 24 or younger at release were arrested, compared to 78.6% of inmates ages 25 to 39 and 69.2% of those age 40 or older.

Punishing someone for a perceived offense against the established rule goes back as far as recorded history and even beyond from archeological and anthropological studies. The Biblical origin of crime and punishment occurred when God drove Adam and Eve out of the Garden of Paradise for dis-obeying his rule. I think the gravity of this transgression must have made a very deep impression on all those that came after because the "sin" of Adam and Eve seems to have had repercussions on all succeeding generations. The concept of justice seems to have been axiomatic in the minds of the ancients as though this was the gold standard of maintaining respect for those in authority since some sort of order was necessary in sustaining any kind of a tribal or community cohesiveness.

The Code of The Code of (King) Hammurabi (1792-1750 BC), of the Babylonian Empire, was perhaps the first official establishment of a set of rules whose obedience was mandatory with punishments relative to a person's status. However, there were those that preceded Hammurabi in establishing rules and laws that governed the behavior of the populace and those that ruled them.

Dominique Charpin, a professor at Ecole Pratique des Hautes Etudes in Paris, writes in his book, "Writing Law and Kingship in Old Babylonian Mesopotamia" (University of Chicago Press, 2010) states that scholars know of the existence of three law codes, set down by kings, that preceded Hammurabi. The oldest was written by a king of Ur whose name was Nammu, who reigned from 2111-2094 BC about 3 centuries before Hammurabi. The 300 laws of Hammurabi discussed a wide range of subjects including homicide, assault, divorce, debt, adoption, tradesman's fees, agricultural practices and even disputes regarding the brewing of beer.

A Master degree thesis extract by A. J. Van Loon of Leiden titled; Law and Order in Ancient Egypt, studied The Development of Criminal Justice from the Pharaonic New Kingdom until the Roman Dominate, reporting the following: In one way or another, the civilization that ruled over Egypt in antiquity could all boast a close connection to the concepts of law and justice, balance and order—all personified by the goddess Ma'at—were cornerstones of Ancient Egyptian religion and society. The Greek Ptolemies, who ruled over Egypt between 323 and 30 BC, would become famous for their advanced and intricate bureaucracy, which also featured a highly effective law enforcement system. The Romans, more than any prided themselves on their laws, which remain influential in societies to this day. This thesis sets out to discover the manner in which criminal justice in Egypt developed from the times of the New Kingdom, through the Ptolemaic era, and under Roman rule. Not only for the above mentioned anecdotal reasons, but also because the capability to deal with crime and to maintain order can serve as an indicator for a successful administration in general. Because criminal law forms an integral part of a legal system in total which, in turn, is inseparable from the general administrative system of a country they all will be taken into account. The following questions are purported to be answered in this thesis:

How were the various legal and administrative systems organized? Which actions were considered to be crimes by the Egyptians, Greeks, and Romans? Who possessed the legal authority to deal with these matters? And, in what manner were criminal transgressions dealt with in practice? In the end, the aim is to not only find out how criminal justice developed during a period of nearly two millennia, but also to offer an explanation as to why these developments took their specific course.

The next significant contribution on issues of crime and punishment came from the Greeks. In 590 BC, down to the emergence of the Roman Empire in the 1st century AD, a popular senate legislator by the name of Draco (thus the expression; Draconian law) established some very severe ordinances regarding the administration of justice which persisted until the advent of Roman ascendency. With the Greeks, however, there emerged a view of law and order tempered by Philosophical perspectives under the scholarship of Socrates, then Plato and finally Aristotle. There was a great deal of intellectual interest in how natural law, as they saw it, would apply not just to the citizens of Greece but to all humans. Certain classes of humans were disbarred from citizenship, however, such as women, immigrants and slaves.

Meanwhile, in China, India and the Far East, punishments were very severe or temperate depending on the immediate persuasion of the Emperor. For example, in China there were "5 punishments" which prevailed from 2070 thru 1600 BCE under the Xi Dynasty. These punishments involved; amputation of a foot or both feet, amputation of a nose, chiseling or tattooing of the face or forehead, removal of reproductive organs and, finally, death. Confucius (551-479 BC), on the other hand, was known for setting ethical models of family and public interactions and setting educational standards and taking a more moderate position on the administration of punishment for transgressions against Imperial law. (Wikipedia)

As we move into the Roman era (27 BC to 480 AD) in the West and up to 1453 AD in the East) legal development spanned over a thousand years of jurisprudence from the Twelve Tables (449 BC) to the Corpus Juris Civilis (529 AD) as ordered by Justinian l. Roman law formed the basic framework for Civil Law in Western Civilization. The Twelve Tables consisted of the following:

I Procedure: for courts and trials
II Trials continued and theft
III Debt

IV Rights of fathers over the family
V Legal guardianship and inheritance Laws
VI Acquisition and possession
VII Land rights and crimes
VIII Torts and delicts (laws of injury)
de IX Public law
X Sacred law

The dictum under Justinian I (529-534 AD) established the Corpus Juris Civilis with: Legislation about religion which mandated the unity of Church and State and anyone not connected to the Christian Church was declared a non-citizen; laws against heresy which declared that all must hold the Christian faith. This served as a springboard for international law and who was under the jurisdiction of the Church; and, against paganism which forbade any pagan practices. All persons present at a pagan sacrifice may be indicted as if for murder. (Wikipedia)

Crime and Punishment under the Emergence of Christianity

This brings us up to the more modern times of the criminal justice system. When we look at the emergence of Western Civilization, we must also look at the father of Christianity, i.e., Judaism and the son of Christianity, i.e., Islam since Christianity emerged from Judaism and Islam emerged from Christianity. It is, also, interesting that the laws pertaining to offensive behavior in all these instances revolved around insults and transgressions against God (Christ being the mediator/savior in Christianity), Yahweh in Judaism and Allah in Islam, rather than against the potentate of civil authority—although in many cases the potentate of a civil jurisdiction was thought of as a god and ruled as such.

So, as we continue with the evolution of criminal jurisprudence in Europe beginning in the 4th century after the Donation of Constantine 1, we see the emergence of the Roman Catholic Church in the West and the Eastern Orthodox Church in the East with institutional dominance in much of the Western and Eastern world. As the Roman Catholic Church gained more power it developed a harsh administrative dominance over "believers" and "non-believers" such as resulted in the Inquisition that started in 1231 when the Pope Gregory IX appointed the first "inquisitor of depravity" to quell the antagonistic heretical movements of the time. There are many interpretations of the extent and characteristics of that era of history. The Catholic Church admits that in France and Spain, particularly, there was a severe threat reaction to the Cathars and Waldensians who opposed the established dogma of the Church as well as the Jews and Moors who, by that time, had established themselves in Spain and attempted to "pass" as Roman Catholics for the protective services of the realm.

One might ask: "Well, what has all this got to do with the point of this essay?" During this period of European history under the sovereignty of the Roman Catholic Papacy, even Kings had to bow down to the Holiness of the Pope and crimes of any kind were considered an affront and insult, not only to the Papacy, but, also, to God Himself and, therefore, crimes of any kind could only be officially admonished and forgiven through the Sacrament of Confession to a priest.

It wasn't until the advent of a Catholic monk by the name of Martin Luther, who in 1517 opposed the Vatican by displaying in public his 95 theses of protest. Also, about this time King Henry VIII of England dissented with Papal rule and sovereignty over another issue of what, one might say, was his own sovereignty and "right" to marry again whom he pleased. In Luther's case it was, what he saw, were the rights of all people to justify themselves in their understanding of Christ and, therefore, God. In King Henry's case it was his insistence to be independent of the rule of the Papacy.

These events seemed to be a watershed time in the History of Western Civilization when the issue of crime and punishment was gradually emerging from crime being thought of as against God but, rather, toward fellow man because an awareness was taking place in the minds of some that moral/ethical responsibilities need not be determined by offenses against the Church but, instead, toward themselves and others. This concept of "self-determination" and the freedom of expression of self during the Renaissance Period from the 14th to the 17th century, appeared to change the course of human history. Probably, the ultimate culmination of this movement was the French Revolution which lasted from 1789 to 1799 in which a populace insurrection occurred to overthrow the absolute sovereignty of the Kingship of France. However, it was the codified Magna Carta (The Great Charter) of June 15, 1215 in England that set down the establishment of the principle that everyone is subject to the law, even kings, and guarantees the rights of individuals, the right to justice and the right to a fair trial. (Wikipedia)

What appeared to be happening during the political history of Europe between the signing of "The Great Charter" and the end of the French Revolution was an emerging awareness of the responsibility of all humans to determine how they shall be ruled—rather than being ruled by obedience to God through the Papacy of the Church, or obedience to a king through a mandate called the "Divine Rights of Kings."

From the 15th through to the 17th centuries there was a great movement to expand the Economic interests of countries like Spain, Portugal, The Netherlands and along with England to explore and colonize foreign lands. In 1492 Christopher Columbus was financed by Ferdinand and Isabella of Spain to explore the riches of, what was then called, "The New World."

There was also an upsurge of zeal among adventurous souls to find a new way of life and liberty and freedom to practice religion and justice as they saw it. New religious persuasion sprang up following the Protestant Revolution that was started by Martin Luther.

The Colonies

When the first pilgrims arrived in Jamestown, VA in 1607 they brought with them the Anglican religion or that of the Church of England, a protestant sect, under King Charles l, along ith the laws of dealing with crime and punishment. There were 12 other colonies established from 1607 in Virginia to Georgia in 1732. Each had their unique political and religious structure pertaining to the administration of punishment for transgressions against the established rules of the community. The community was established by the Virginia Company of London and was characterized by strict civil and religious codes of punishment such as:

For cause of undeserved death, the punishment of starving, hanging, burning, breakage upon the wheel.

For running to the Indians to help the punishment of burning.

For stealing to satisfy hunger the punishment of hanging from a tree or chained to a tree for starving, whipping, working as a slave in irons.

Contributor: Colonial Crimes and Punishment, James A Cox

The second colony established was New Hampshire in 1629. The colony was founded by Capt. John Mason and the Rev. John Millwright who promoted industries of potatoes, fishing, textiles and ship building. Puritanism was the primary religion but eventually gave way to the Congregational church which included the beliefs of the Quakers and the Baptists- The Puritans led strict religious lives, and dissenters were treated harshly. Then, in 1689, the English Parliament passed the Tolerant Act, which stopped corporal punishment for dissenters, such as cropping the ears of Quakers and whippings for Baptists. This act also freed other religious persuasions to establish churches in Puritan colonies without punishment.

The third colony to be in, what was called New England, was the charter colony of Massachusetts Bay in 1630. The Puritans established a theocratic government with the franchise limited to church members only. The Rev. John Cotton and others sought vigorously to prevent independence of other religious views. Puritans sought to "purify" the Church of England from its "Catholic" practices, maintaining that the Church of England was only partially reformed.

The Massachusetts Bay colony was also noted for prosecuting crimes of moral offenses more so than crimes against persons or property. Crimes against the government were more severe against people of lower status and individuals with black skin were thought to be strange and exotic, evil and satanic creatures and were treated mercilessly. (Contributor: Crime and Punishment in Colonial Times—Robert C. Twombly and Robert H. Moore, Apr. 1967)

The next colony to be established among the 13 original was Maryland in 1632. The intent of Lord Baltimore was to provide a safe haven for English Catholics in the New World at the time of the European wars of religious strife among Anglicans, Puritans, Catholics and Quakers. Lord Baltimore was later removed and replaced by a Protestant, Charles Calvert. As in all other jurisdictions of colonial policy there was always an undertone of religious moral transgression and such transgressions were deemed to be a severe threat to the stability and integrity of the community.

Both Connecticut and Rhode Island were established in 1636 as charter colonies. In both cases a group of people were led by such as Roger Williams who purchased land from the Narragansett Indians to establish the Rhode Island colony in Providence. A similar situation occurred with Connecticut. The rules and ordinances were similar in that such were administered with guidelines set up by religious factions. In this case it was also of the Puritan persuasion. The remaining six colonies of: Delaware in 1638, Carolina in 1653, New Jersey and New York in 1664, Pennsylvania in 1682 and Georgia in 1732 had similar beginnings with very harshly imposed punishments under the aegis of the religious constabulary.

However, since religiosity in the administration of justice tended to be rather severe and debilitating there were undercurrents of discontent that eventually found its way into our Constitution and Bill of Rights which stressed the separation of Church and State following the American Revolutionary War of 1776.

The Development of Criminal Justice in America

As a result, the notion of imprisonment and separation from society became a more enlightened approach to the administration of crime and punishment along with the prospect of correction—but that has not shown to be an effective solution with reference to the great recidivism rate in America, today.

The great question, then, seems to be: *How can we as a progressive and vital society deal with those who transgress our peace and order? How can justice be administered humanely and with an understanding that will enable one so disinclined toward amiable society with his fellow man to be truly reset on a more viable course of life?*

In the 19th century there emerged the "due process model" and the "crime control model." The origin of the due process model originally came from clause 39 of the Magna Carta in which "No man shall be arrested or imprisoned except by lawful judgment of his peers or the law of the land." The "crime control model" on the other hand, allegedly began with the origin of the first modern police force with the Metropolitan Police Force in London in 1829 by Sir Robert Peel. The Peelian Principles, as they were called, were developed as a deterrent to urban crime and disorder. This was followed in the U.S. in 1838 in which Boston and then New York City in 1844 followed suit. However, the police were not respected because corruption was rampant.

In 1920 in Berkeley, California police chief August Vollmer and OSW. Wilson began to professionalize, adopt new technologies and place emphasis on training and professional qualifications of new hires. (Wikipedia)

The "crime control model" refers to a theory of criminal justice which places emphasis on reducing crime in society through increased police and prosecutorial powers. In contrast, the "due process model" focuses on individual liberties and rights and is concerned with limiting the powers of government. We can, therefore, see that behind this political fugue was the conflict between self-determination and "police" powers of the King and the Papacy in Europe. This dichotomous way of thinking (due process vs crime control models) with respect to criminal behavior presented, in practice, as the legalities, on the one hand, and the administration of justice on the other.

As the population in the U.S. grew and the incidence of crime also increased the court dockets expanded to an unmanageable level and "a fast and speedy trial" was no longer feasible. As a result, plea bargaining has served as compensatory dispositions—even in some serious cases–by reducing a felony to a misdemeanor. Moreover, the courts are literally overwhelmed with those being brought to trial for drug abuse problems and crimes associated with it. Police are overwhelmed because of the sheer volume and seriousness of criminal behavior. The police also get frustrated because so often those who risk their lives to apprehend criminal offenders find that the offenders are soon released from custody and back on the streets.

As a former deputy juvenile probation officer, myself, in 1960 1 have seen the character of crime committed by juvenile go from petty theft, malicious mischief and joy riding to carrying guns and knives to school and, in some cases, using these weapons against fellow students and even teachers. The precursor to more serious crimes on the part of juveniles were those cases called "beyond the control and supervision" of parents because parents were too busy struggling to earn a living and consequently relinquished their authority to the school, the church and any other institution that was mandated by law to step in——including the juvenile probation officer. Parents would often come into the office saying, "1 get no respect from my kid. He won't listen to me and won't obey me. You (the juvenile probation officer) take charge." When children do not get the attention and developmental support they need, it becomes axiomatic that they would get into trouble with the law or with themselves. Psychologists will say that when the emotional needs of children are not met, they will either act out against society (usually in groups or gangs) or against themselves in mental/emotional disorders or self-mutilation. When this all happened in the 60s the result was the great juvenile/tribal movement which opened the door to the massive drug and homeless problems that we had not seen before. This was the era of "tune in, turn on and drop out," as promoted by the Harvard psychology professor, Timothy Leary.

Educational standards have declined relative to the demand for increased competitiveness in the technical global market place resulting in fewer young people being prepared for adult responsibilities. Many juveniles have landed in custody because they have chosen to resort to the hopeful multiple contexts—in families, schools, peer groups, baseball teams, religious organizations, and many other groups—and each context is a potential source of protective factor as well as risks. These children demonstrate that children are protected not only by the self-righting nature of development, but also by the actions of adults, by their own actions, by the nurturing of their assets, by opportunities to succeed and by the experiences of success. The behavior of adults often plays a critical role in children's risks, resources, opportunities and resilience. Development is biased toward competence, but there is no such thing as an invulnerable child. If we allow the prevalence of known risk factors development to rise while resources for children fall, we can expect the competence of individual children and the human capital of the nation to suffer."

Jeremy Glenesk, studied Criminal Justice in several countries around the world, at Mount Royal University in Calgary, Alberta, and in Feb. 2016 he presented his findings as follows:

"Norway is considered (there is some debate, due to varying systems of measurement worldwide because some agencies define recidivism as re-arrest while others look at a new conviction upon release) to have one of, if not the lowest recidivism rates in the world. Why is this? Many would argue that their system works so well because they treat offenders as actual people, rather than as a tumor that needs to be excised from society. You can find plenty of articles on Google, and pictures of their prisons, and many people from other nations would laugh and think it's a joke.

Their prisons are pristine. They look like a country club. Offenders in some Norwegian prisons can go horseback riding, and often have televisions, gyms, and kitchens. Their system seeks to remove their freedom, and nothing else. They live a healthy and normal lifestyle while in prison, but are simply unable to leave. Their system seeks to actively rehabilitate offenders back into society by teaching them skills and finding them work upon reentry into society."

I might add that this way of thinking uses a reward system as a motivator rather than punishment. Prisoners are deprived of privileges for non-compliance and rewarded with special privileges for compliance and acceptable contributions to the wellbeing of all.

"So how does Norway accomplish this feat? The country relies on a concept called 'restorative justice', which aims to repair the harm caused by crime rather than punish people. This system focuses on rehabilitating prisoners. Taking a look at Halden Prison you'll see what we mean. The 75-acre facility maintains as much 'normalcy' as possible. That means no bars on the widows, kitchens fully equipped with sharp objects, and friendships between guards and inmates. For Norway, removing people's freedom is enough of a punishment." And the fact that the recidivism rate is so low testifies to the fact that freedom is more valued than incarceration—even with the best of living conditions.

"The maximum life sentence is 21 years with 5-year extensions for special cases if the prisoner does not accept rehabilitation. As Are Hoidel, Halden's Prison director puts it: Our goal is that every inmate in Norwegian prison is going back to society. Do you want people who are angry—or people who are rehabilitated?"

It could be argued that those who are the most intractable are those who have experienced extreme emotional deprivation as small children and, consequently, never learned to trust or see the world as a friendly place. Question: Is it possible to re-generate trust in an adult whose character has been formed without it?

A suggestion that, on the face of it, sounds barbaric, cruel and unusual punishment might, on second thought, seem more humane when looked at from the point of view of true rehabilitation. When someone develops cataracts of the eyes and loses vision an ophthalmologist will remove the diseased lens and then replace them with artificial ones which restores vision. If one were to remain without the lenses for a time they would be required to depend on or trust someone in order to exercise any effective ambulation. With those without criminal records getting around is a laborious task even with a seeing eye dog—and their freedoms are considerably curtailed. With someone who is imprisoned having lost their vision but with the hope of regaining it again could serve as a strong motivational reward for attitude readjustment Perhaps the pros and cons of such an idea could be the subject of serious discussion among those whose job it is to truly rehabilitate prisoners.

On Elemental Cause/Effect Relationships

Since this essay is about addressing the problem of not only recidivism in the U.S. criminal justice system but the incidence of crime and violence in the society in general—and why some people are inclined toward crime and social disorder in the first place.

Referring to a study written up by Denise C. Gottfredson, David B. Wilson and Stacy Skroban Najaka titled; Evidence-Based Crime Prevention-School Based Crime Prevention, published by Routledge in 2002 we have the following findings:

"Schools have great potential as a locus for crime prevention. They provide regular access to students throughout the developmental years, and perhaps the only consistent access to large numbers of the most crime-prone young children in the early school years. The schools are staffed with individuals paid to help youth develop as healthy, happy, productive citizens and the community usually supports schools' efforts to socialize youth."

Factors which are considered precursors of delinquency as identified by research are the following: Characteristics of school and classroom related environments as well as individual-related school-related experiences, personal values, attitudes and beliefs.

School environmental factors related to delinquency include availability of drugs, alcohol and weapons. School related experiences and attitudes which often precede delinquency, include poor school performance and attendance, low feeling of attachment to the school and education at all. Other contributing actors are: Peer rejection, bullying, impulsiveness and associating with delinquent peers and a pervading low self-esteem.

Individual factors contributing toward delinquent behavior are rebellious attitudes and beliefs favoring law violations and low levels of social competency skills such as identifying likely consequences of choices.

In addressing the problem of improving the school experience as a corrective approach to the growing phenomenon of crime and disorder in our society we must look at the three most important institutions for raising healthy, happy and purposeful children: The family, the school and the neighborhood or community. There is ample evidence-based research to support this contention. If we want to preserve our way of life, we must focus on the progeny of America—those who will take over after each generation.

The Family as a Bulwark Against Delinquency and Social Disorder

Nothing beats an emotionally warm, stable and attentive home for the successful rearing of children. The quality of parenting in the U.S. appears to have declined in the last 50 years or so. This is partly due to economic and political changes as well as the advent of social diversions. There was a time after WWII when a young father was able to get a secure job which paid enough to support his family with a house, a car and enough money for health services and recreation and even to offer helping support for tuitions that were exceeding affordable. Mothers were able to stay home and attend to the needs and character building of their small children and there was mutual support between parents and teachers. This is no longer the case today since most young parents must both works, even if there are two parents in the home which often is not the case, just to make ends meet. The children often go unsupervised and neglected. Stability in the home is now available to only a few who are fortunate enough to be highly endowed with wealth. Higher education, today, is virtually prohibited for many of the deserving young people because of inordinate costs.

Youngsters need all the elements of security mentioned above by Maslow, Erikson, Masten and Coatsworth and others whose studies clearly show that elements of growth and maturity follow the pattern of gratification and achievement of needs, developmental tasks and competency. Parents need to be mature and competent, themselves, so they can provide the environmental and emotional structure that will foster healthy development.

The following is a parable of a boy named Mitch who was like any precious, incomparable child, a million-dollar diamond in the rough.

For the first few years of his life, Mitch only knew himself from the reflections he saw of himself in the eyes of his caretakers. Even though his caretakers were not blind they saw him through the kaleidoscope of their own perceptions, needs and expectations. Consequently, even though his caretakers were always present, not one of them ever actually saw him as he was as he attempted to emerge as the person he was meant to be. By the time he was grown he knew himself only as a mosaic of other people's images of him. No one had ever really seen him or mirrored back to him who he really was or looked like. As a result, he thought he was the mosaic of images. Sometimes in the dark of night when he was all alone, Mitch knew that something of profound importance was missing. He experienced a gnawing sense of emptiness—a deep void. He tried to fill the emptiness and void with many things: accomplishments, money, status, prestige, food, sex, adventure, travel, marriages, children, excitement, work—even exercise. But no matter what he did he never felt the gnawing emptiness go away. In the quiet of the night when all the distractions were gone, he heard a still quiet voice that said: "Don't forget; please don't forget me!" But alas! Mitch did forget and went to his death never knowing who he was This is the tragic story of those who are raised by incompetent parents or caregivers.

How children perceive themselves and the world depends so much on how people close to them relate to them. A case in point is the FLDS cult presided over by Warren Jeffs (who had numerous wives and children and claimed to be a prophet) who was convicted and imprisoned in 2011 on two felony counts of child sexual assault—and even to this day he controls his cult members from within his prison cell.

There was a time in our history when children were produced and exploited primarily to help with the economic security of the family or to be exploited by commercial industry and we have come to recognize that this was an unjust exploitation of the child. Children have rights as well as adults. They have a right to "life, liberty and their own pursuit of happiness" as stated in our own Constitution. They have a right to be respected and honored and taught that in our society, which is a democratic republic, that each person has a responsibility toward themselves and to others in the sustaining and perpetuation of this way of life. With rights go privileges and, also, responsibilities. The responsibilities we talk of speak to the importance and value of developing one's potential capabilities so they can enjoy the satisfaction that comes with successful accomplishment for themselves and, also, the inherent gratification and gratitude that comes from serving others with what you have to offer. Parents need to spend enough time with their children so they can enjoy them and be sensitive enough to reflect back to them what interests excites them. In other words, parents must be emotionally supportive with their children while, at the same time, making sure children learn to do for themselves and strive for confident independence. That's the job of parents. A highly recommended book in how to inspire values in children is: Children Learn What They Live by Dorothy Law Nolte. For example, she writes: "If children live with criticism, they learn to condemn— If children live with acceptance, they learn to love."

It is the contention of many that the rights of children are severely violated and grave injustice is done when children are produced by the irresponsible and immature. It is for this reason that much more ought to be done in the schools and by parents in teaching the responsibilities and hardships of parenthood as well as the delights and satisfactions of raising a child. I would go so far as to advocate that prospective parents be given formal tests to determine if they are qualified for parenthood. We test for admittance to special schools and higher education, for police and public safety, for driving, we test for qualifying professional people and just about everything except the most important function of our society—the raising of children.

The School as a Bulwark Against Delinquency and Social Disorder

When a child first enters the school system it is now possible to give each child a thorough and comprehensive evaluation—not only for readiness for school but also an assessment of the child health and developmental milestones, social and domestic background and any other factors that would deter from the child being able to successfully matriculate into the educational process. This is the time in a child's life when it is so important for teachers and parents to be sensitive to any pathological traits that may be developing in a child. This is the time when corrective measures can be most effective. We wonder why some individuals in a fit of rage will cause terrible violence and destruction as an adult. It is the result of accumulated distress over years of unfulfilled needs and gratifications during the developmental years. Addressing the needs of these young people at the early stage of their development is, to a large extent, the work of the professional school psychologist assisted by the primary caregivers, school personnel and other professionals.

It would also be suggested that the grades from k through 3 be ungraded so that children can be entered at their readiness levels, be individualized by the teacher and remain so until ready for 4th grade. Some children are ready at 4 and others not until they are 6. Furthermore, even though competition is a valued endeavor in our society it is not productive for very small children to feel they are competing with other children for grades or recognition. They must only be encouraged to excel at whatever they show an interest and propensity for. In other words, to compete with themselves in attempting to master whatever they do. In addition, grading should not be competitive at the early stages of development. So, instead of an a, b, c, d, f grading system a grading system of pass, superior or incomplete should be adopted as recommended by William Glasser in his book, Schools Without Failure. Those with special gifts ought to be encouraged to do special projects that they want to do and present their results to the class instead of advancing beyond their peers and classmates. Advancement, if necessary, can be done at higher grade levels if warranted. In this regard it is also important that those who are gifted be recognized and dealt with accordingly so as not to stifle their inherent intensity, complexity and drive.

Early school experiences for a child are very important in setting a lifelong attitude toward education and learning and that is why the teachers at those lower levels must be specially trained and qualified not only in teaching skills for small children but knowledge of the pedagogy of child development. A hyper-critical teacher can severely dampen the natural enthusiasm for learning. A warm, intelligent and encouraging teacher can make all the difference in the development of a child's attitude toward learning and toward his/her own self-concept of competence. We want to be sure that each child, by the time he/she finishes those early 4 years (K3) is well grounded in the basics of reading, writing and arithmetic and successful socialization.

When a child enters 4th grade, this is the time to start introducing the elements of the immediate community (the services of the police, firefighters, libraries, medical personnel and all those connected with public service) in which he/she lives and extending that to the broad concept of nationhood and, for that matter, the world community at large. Also, the reality of competitiveness as an incentive toward excellence in production and self-development can be introduced as an assertive disposition—not as a hostile or aggressive attitude. There should never be hostile/competitive bullying or discrimination prejudices in the schools. Problems like this ought to be handled by the school counselor. Sadly, many schools are unequipped with well trained counselors. Unfortunately, counselors are often frustrated by being assigned administrative tasks that occupy much of their time.

Formal curricula in many schools are sadly lacking in not only socialization skills but in the practical aspects of living. This, it seems to me, is an important part of educating the young in their progress toward adulthood. In other words, "why reinvent the wheel," as the old saying goes. Why not give children a heads-up on how to matriculate into the adult world? Let's give them the benefit of our experience and what we have learned as adults.

At the high school level, much more emphasis ought to be placed in a child's endeavor to successfully achieve the developmental task of identity and social competence. This is where the services of the professional counselor become so important. In addition to the basic subjects of the high school curriculum the teen-ager must come to know who they are and how to relate themselves to the "world of work" and the adult world in general. It is a very complex and competitive world they are about to inherit and they should be given the knowledge and skills necessary to navigate successfully in this modern world of today. They must know about how to form effective and meaningful relationships, how to make their contribution to their society, how to handle their money and negotiate through the complex world of finance and housing, how to take care of their health and wellbeing as they grow older and how to deal with discouragement and failure and that will inevitably happen as well. There ought to be discussions about values—not just one's own but those of the society and world in which they live so they can make some choices about what works and what doesn't. As adults they are going to have to make choices about how and where they want to live and work, who they want to mate with, who they want to lead them and how they want their economy to run. These are all very practical questions that teen-agers want answered. Without this guidance it becomes a very anxious and depressing outlook for their future.

In our educational history teachers were respected and admired members of the community. They were regarded as professionals and the respect was relayed through the parents by their children and when a child was reprimanded in the school the parent often backed up the teacher unless there was some blatant misbehavior on the part of the school official. In that case the educator was either reprimanded or dismissed before the advent of tenure. The issue of tenure has many pros and cons but the abuses can have serious consequences for good teachers and the quality of education for children.

Many of us including school officials themselves attest that tenure in the lower grades poses complex problems because it serves as a haven for incompetent and uninspired people who do not have the talent or inspiration to be a quality teacher. This has a detrimental effect on the morale of good teachers and it seriously hampers the effectiveness of a child's educational experience. Tenure at the college or university level made some sense because it was thought that people at that level of education were mature enough to use their own judgment as to the ideas and persuasions of their professors because professors ought to have the freedom to express their own opinions and thoughts. However, the younger students are still in the process of developing their characters and therefore it is imperative that teachers be more concerned about teaching the fundamental values and purposes of this nation as well as what this nation stands for. Too many children, today, are very unclear as to what this nation does stand for.

Young people have a great deal of idealism and enthusiasm and, also a desire to assume some meaningful responsibility. This, also, ought to be part of the high school program in which seniors have the opportunity to engage in a work/study experience of their liking so they can learn, under supervision, what it is like to actually hold a job and come to work on time. This can be a supplemental activity for half a day. I did this in Brazil when I was the guidance counselor at an American school in Recife and it worked out well.

I am also persuaded that, in terms of student morale and self-respect, the school ought to establish not only rules of conduct, but rules of dress and rules pertaining to driving cars to school. Driving a car is a privilege, not a right and ought to be regarded as such by the school administration so this ought to be a Senior privilege particularly if he/she has responsibilities that warrant the use of a car. Students as well as teachers must have a healthy respect for themselves and their institution of learning.

An old axiom among psychologists is that you can't start solving a problem until you first acknowledge that it exists. With reference to the school systems in America it does appear that there is a resistance to acknowledging shortcomings and making changes that will adapt to the challenges of the 21st century. In the past children were regimented into a lock-step rote learning mode that was suitable for employment in a manufacturing economy. A worker could offer his skills with loyalty to a company and be well assured of a job throughout his working life with a gold watch and reliable pension upon retirement. That type of employment is becoming rare and the schools must be re-configured to meet the skill demands of the 21st century labor market. The world is becoming more interactive and complex every day. In order for a democratic republic like ours to prevail the populace must be educated to understand the real issues confronting the society.

Since education is also a matter of building character in the young it is important that teachers and educators meet higher professional standards of effectiveness—much like all professions. That would include such qualities as creating a friendly classroom atmosphere, establishing a feeling of security, exerting a stabilizing influence, inspiring originality and initiative and developing self-reliance.

Tenure at the primary/elementary and secondary levels ought to be re-considered for the sake of keeping an edge on the effectiveness of teachers and ensuring that those who are not in keeping with standards of excellence should be let go and guided toward other occupations more suitable to their interests and skills.

The public school system must re-dedicate itself to the noble purpose of enhancing communal attitudes of good will and connectedness and building confidence and trust in the American way of life. Community leaders must promote social-ethical values in the workplace such as flextime, in-house child care, maternity and paternity leave, counseling for those that must be re-assigned or have need for resolving personal crises, work-out facilities and healthy lunch counters. In addition, coordinating with the high schools in the process of matriculating young people into the labor market so they can be assured of suitable training and direction in the interests of a more synergistic work environment is an absolute necessity.

Children must be educated from a wider perspective taking into account the whole range of community activities. Schools ought to be kept open much as libraries are (or should be) to serve as resources for community problem solving and after school activities. The public schools are the only institutional establishment that can ensure an educated populace for the perpetuity of a democratic-republic society and serve as an opportunity for each individual to cultivate their best aspirations and dreams.

The Community as a Bulwark Against Delinquency and Social Disorder

As I mentioned at the beginning of this essay, the tribal instinct is in all of us going back to as far back as the Anthropologists have studied. This primitive instinct is what binds us into units as small as the family and as large as nationhood. In recent times the world populace is seeing itself as a theater of "globalization" which means that our concept of tribalization is, at least in an economical sense, becoming widespread internationally.

However, getting back to smaller details we must look at our communities and neighborhoods as a bulwark against delinquency and social disorder. In many areas of our nation, families and schools are not well secured and provide only marginal support for children growing up. Great volunteer services are needed and are, indeed, available in most communities such as the Police Athletic League, Midnight basketball, CASA (Court Appointed Special Advocate) program and many volunteer services for youth offered by churches and ancillary school activities. Anything that will help interface young people with local community resources and enlist their own services will inspire a young person to value him or herself—and that is important.

Also, there are volunteer services for young people to offer their skills and energy in such activities as: distributing Goodwill clothing to those less fortunate along with toys and stuffed animals, sending off packages and cards to the military deployed, texting about political concerns to local representatives, collecting books for children who can't afford them as well as those who are hospitalized, helping to tutor those who are struggling with the language, raking leaves for the elderly, teaching computer skills to the elderly, taking people on tours of historic sites, volunteering to coach or referee at children's sports events, bake sales for charity and many more. The idea is to get young people interested in exploring their own inner resources to enhance their sense of value and contribution. It is all about instilling young people with the feeling of being an important and useful member of the Tribe.

Though there has been an insidious erosion of community trust and confidence in government and social processes in the past 40 or 50 years, those of the WWII era will often say that during the great world war this nation pulled together and worked together as a united community with a common purpose of survival. That sense of communality and common purpose can and must be regained but without the conditions of war. That is the great challenge of the future and we can succeed if we want to. Most humans, it is largely agreed, desire a living environment that values a sense of cooperation and good will rather than mistrust and alienation, a sense of community built on a common noble purpose rather than social estrangement and isolation.

Maybe we have focused too much on the seductive powers of liberty and freedom and basic civil rights for individuals without attaching the true quality of those virtues to the concept of social responsibility. There may not be, in reality, a true quality of liberty, freedom, justice or rights without a sense of social responsibility and connectedness. Whether it be on an individual basis or on a societal basis and whether it be in the field of education, law, medicine, business, industry or politics, the society, as a whole, may be thwarted in its destined greatness unless all of us espouse the traditional values of social integrity that this country was founded upon. That is the crossing we all must make in order to feel re-connected to a noble national purpose and an ever-unfolding bright destiny.

The way people rallied around those who were so devastated by the Oklahoma City bombing of 1995 and the wonderful acts of courage and compassion that came from all parts of this country ought to serve as an inspiration. It goes to show that the American people still possess that indefatigable character and social integrity that served us well in all the great crises of the nation's history. In spite of all the indulgences of the past 50 years we do live in a world of renewed hope. In the past 50 years we all lived with the terrible possibility of global nuclear destruction.

The world has now seen the demise of the Communist Soviet Union. There is international agreement that it is in everyone's interest to contain and control the proliferation of nuclear weapons. Those dreaded missiles are no longer the global threat as before except perhaps for a small number of renegade countries who might wish to endorse terrorism for their own interests and even, they can be dissuaded from evil intent. The United Nations is finding its role in the world and helping to maintain a fragile peace in the tangled division of the former Yugoslavia and the Middle East. Continuing advances in medical technologies and pharmacology along with technical achievements and computerization have revolutionized life on this planet and promises a brighter future of greater need gratification for all peoples of the earth—thereby laying the groundwork for more effective cooperation and problem solving among the peoples of the earth.

Perhaps now, if we can responsibly address our problems at home, we may begin to look optimistically to the future with confidence to build and create rather than destroy, to enter an era of mutually assured cooperation rather than "mutually assured destruction," to educate and train rather than indulge in "projects" of despair.

There now appears to be an emerging consciousness of the implications of social/ethical values in the workplace and the need to recognize the importance of human considerations in modern living. Some of the great corporations in the U.S. are discovering that it is in their best interests to provide consideration for such human needs as flex time, in home child care, maternity and/or paternity leave, counseling for those who must be reassigned to have need for resolving personal crises, work-out facilities and healthy lunch counters, coordinating with high schools in the process of matriculating young people into the labor market and assuring that they are suitably trained and directed—and a generally more socially synergistic work environment. It is becoming more apparent that a need gratified employee is a more productive employee who can cope more effectively with the demands of the ever-increasing technologies.

The people's righteous anger is rising against the forces of impotence and negativity and, as has been the case in the past, when the American people are provoked to justifiable anger the Ship of State will be reset on its true course while new technological systems and viable cultural values will assume a direction of purpose and thoughtful intention. There does appear to be changes in the wind There is a new and exciting concept in education that does not yet have a full consensus of the American people but it is growing in strength in various areas of the U.S. It is characterized by an integration of the community and the school in a more dynamic and synergistic way. It stresses a melding of school and various community resources. It brings into focus the needs of educating children from a wider perspective, i.e., from the point of view of involved parents, educators, community policing and law, medical and mental health workers, and those in business and industry. Schools under the new system would be kept open as channels for learning and community problem solving such as libraries are kept open (or ought to be) to the public as resource facilities and used for children's after school activities. Older, retired people would be brought into the schools as surrogate grandparents to offer emotional as well as educational support.

Promoting a revival of the American hope for the future and the revitalization of the society is by a whole-hearted support of three of society's most important institutions: the family, the public school and the community. In the final analysis, it is not a question of whether or not the public school system can be saved. It must be saved otherwise the society will be dominated by an economic and educational elite. The public school system is the only institution that assures a broadly based educated populace as this democratic republic requires so that it may maintain and enhance itself in perpetuity. I say let the focus for renewal first be placed upon the schools and the neighborhoods of those schools because that is where the hopes and dreams of parents through their children can begin to move in an upward direction. The public schools are where the minds, bodies and spirits of the children of America can be molded with strengths and faith for the future. It is also the place in which real opportunity and independence can be fostered through the acquisition of life and workplace skills and self-understanding. Let us think, therefore, of hope for the future through opportunity in the public school system as the key concept of American education. We only need to give it a new vitality and enthusiasm. I believe the United States has a unique destiny to become a beacon of light to the world but we are letting that precious beacon grow dim. Let us stand on the side of light rather than darkness.

All this, I believe, will serve the interest of improving the criminal justice system in America and move in the direction of saving human resources rather than warehousing in a penal system that demonstrably does not work—and, also, reducing violence and despair in America as a way of life.

Part III

Reforming a New America

At this time, in the summer of 2012, the U.S. is coming to another "crossing of the Rubicon" and it is believed that history from now on will mark this period as the sad demise of a great and promising new Republic or the beginning of an innovative and re-creative new adventure in hopeful and purposeful living.

In his book, "Come Home, America, The Rise and Fall (And Redeeming Promise) of Our Country," William Greider quotes Adam Smith, founder of modern market economics, who was on the side of compassion. Greider goes on to say that Smith was revered by Economists for describing "the invisible hand" of the marketplace and taught that "moral sentiments"—human acts of "fellow feeling"—are the guiding forces that govern economics and prevent markets from injuring society. He further describes that empathy for others, self-interested mutuality, and other moral verities—are the things that

Adam Smith taught (and most modern economists ignore).

For many years now government and private corporations have been ignoring these ideals of our early American history and collaborating to skew our society in the direction of a bifurcated populace of the extremely wealthy and the extremely impoverished. According to author Holly Sklar, the average wage for full-time workers in 1982 was $34,199.00 in comparison (buying power) with 2006 dollars. In 2007, twenty-five years later, the average wage for full-time workers was $34, 861.00.

On the other hand, in 1982 when Forbes magazine first published its annual list of the four hundred richest Americans, there were only thirteen billionaires among them. Twenty-five years later, the Forbes 400 consisted entirely of billionaires and eighty-two were left off the 2007 list because they were not rich enough to make the cut. This great divergence of wealth is why families have had to take on extraordinary levels of debt as they try to stay afloat and keep up with mortgage payments when their incomes are no longer rising. In 2005, US household savings went negative–people spent more than they earned–for the first time since 1933.

Since Barack Obama was elected in 2008, his administration has been dedicated to restoring a balance between conservative and liberal persuasions, but the

Republican Party from the start has cast accusations that he is moving the country toward Socialism and they have opposed every significant bill advanced by President Obama or the Democratic majority. However, these criticisms dissolve under the most rudimentary examination of the facts. Firstly, Sam Tanenhaus, in his recent book, "The Death of Conservatism," has stated that the decision of Obama's team to fortify the banking system and improve the flow of credit is, unequivocally, an attempt to salvage the free market. Fearful allegations that bailing out GM would result in nationalizing the auto industry had proven false. Secondly, Obama's plan to extend health coverage to the nearly fifty million Americans who lack it is no more socialist than providing Medicare for citizens over the age of 65. In Obama's first year, it was no longer enough to oppose Obama's health-care reform bill. They warned that it was a federal "take-over" and the Speaker of the House, John Boehner, recently commented that the entire Obama health care law ought to be "taken out by the roots." At a town-hall meeting, Bob Inglis, a House Republican from South Carolina, was besieged by angry constituents. One said, "Keep your hands off my Medicare." Inglis replied, "Actually, sir, your health care is being provided by the government." And thirdly, Obama's foreign policy premised on diplomacy and multilateral concord, is as forceful a repudiation of the imperial presidency as we have seen in the modern era.

All these are the actions of a leader who, while politically liberal, is temperamentally conservative and who has placed his faith in the durability—and renewability—of American institutions.

Another example of the oppositional attitude of the Republicans in the Congress, it should be pointed out, is that in 2009 the Republicans objected that the Obama stimulus plan offered too little help to small businesses. But when Obama, conceding the point, proposed an infusion of $30 billion to those businesses, with the sum drawn from TARP (troubled asset relief program) funds, Republicans instantly ridiculed the plan for no apparent reason other than to deny Obama a victory. The message of the Republicans is sheer stridency and opposition. Accusations that Obama is a covert socialist were made by Newt Gingrich and Rush Limbaugh in the Conservative Political Action Conference in February of 2009. When the group reconvened the following year, it was Glenn Beck who summarized the latest version of the movement by saying that, "Progressivism is the cancer in America." He went on to say that the Democrats were "liberal neo monarchists" and "would kill the very spirit that has built the nation." Where are the reasonable conservatives today? Robert Taft believed in taking a stance of opposition and criticism although he supported Social Security and public housing and—overcoming his isolationist principles—approved both NATO and the Marshall Plan.

There is so much dissention today in our Congress with so little meaningful legislation. It is almost as though most Americans are resigned to an ever-declining Nation with little hope of a resurgence of spirit and optimism. There is an oft quoted analogy of the frog that jumps into a pot of water. The frog is unaware that the temperature of the water is gradually rising and he adapts to the increasing heat until he suddenly realizes that the heat will kill him if he doesn't get out but by this time, he is so weak he doesn't have the strength to save himself. I don't think this analogy holds up for Americans because any society of people who could summon the energy and communal effort, almost overnight, as they did during WWII to meet the challenge of survival can summon, again, the will and determination to capture the wind and set the luffing Ship of State on its intended course.

The following are a few ideas gleaned from many sources mentioned in the "Reading Material" list at the end of this essay:

"Only a single payer system of national health care can save what we estimate is the $350 billion wasted annually on medical bureaucracy and redirect those funds to expand coverage,"

Himmelstein and Woolhandler
wrote in the New York Times.

Other nations have demonstrated that a nationalized system puts a lid on prices and profits, the main source of the perennial inflation of health care costs. The U.S. approach, in contrast to other successful health care systems, rewards the private sector and punishes the customers. The adversaries, to this concept of health service rather than health insurance, object because they think it is "socialistic." This is a gross distortion of reality by catastrophizing systems that provide services and support for all the people without disturbing the entrepreneurship of those who stimulate the industry and business of the country. Admittedly, the initial cost of a conversion would be considerable, but less than Washington quickly spent on rescuing Wall Street firms. An estimated saving would be $30 billion a year. It is interesting to note that during WWII and by 1946 the accumulated government debt had reached 120% of the GDR Many people thought the nation would collapse under the weight of its debt and feared it would slide back into a depression. However, the opposite turned out to be true. After the war, the post-war economy expanded greatly and launched the most successful recovery the world had ever seen. This was accomplished, in large part, by all the investment in new factories and new technologies and instituting the "socialistic" GI Bill that allowed returning veterans to go to college and support the emergence of a stronger middle class. So, as WWII demonstrated, the reality test is not the size of the federal budget but whether the borrowed money is invested for the future.

The pension system is in very poor working order. This nation lives with an extraordinary contradiction. In an era when financial wealth has grown explosively, millions of baby boomers now find themselves approaching retirement with paltry savings and no pensions. They will have to keep working into their old age or accept a sharp drop in their standard of living. Social Security, the bedrock insurance for the elderly, provides income equivalent to the federal minimum wage. The old-style corporate pensions that guaranteed retirement benefits are fast disappearing as companies shed them to boost their profits. However, we can look to the many successful models. The Pension Rights Center proposes doing a lot of readjusting of the 401 (K) system. A proposal was made for a new and inclusive national pension that alongside Social Security would require all employees to save in exchange for guaranteed portable individual pension accounts that would pay up to 70% of pre-retirement earnings. Furthermore, there are many successful models that use this approach and provide stable, reliable retirement benefits, including low-overhead, non-profit administrators with no game playing and no profiteering. Examples include mandatory TIAA-CREF pensions for college professors, the construction trades, multiemployer pension plans jointly managed by labor and management, foreign systems like Australia's new national pension system, and the U.S. government's own Thrift Savings Plan for federal employees.

Restoring just taxation is a moral cause, but also a major step toward financing big changes in society. A direct tax on wealth is considered unacceptable in American politics because it is said it amounts to "confiscation" of private property. However, homeowners pay a "wealth tax" every year at the local and state levels–the property tax on their homes–and no one calls it confiscatory. The largest wealth holders and financial institutions could be offered a choice–either pay a modest wealth tax to the government or invest the equivalent in a list of innovative priority ventures or public improvements. There are so many ways to make significant changes and improvements in American political society and we must ask ourselves if the status quo is really what we want for the future of our country. The point is that the nation must mobilize capital to undertake hundreds or thousands of large-scale, long-term projects to bring the unemployment rate down, provide substantial jobs and invest in the future with structural reconstruction.

Many people strongly objected to FDR's administration because they thought he seized too much executive power and with all his projects was moving the country toward socialism. The fact is that his administration set the stage for a victory over the Axis powers during World War Il and a substantial economic recovery after the war. FDR enumerated a list of "rights" that would for many years be the textbook for political reform and social advancement. They included the following:

- The right to a useful and remunerative job;

- The right to earn enough to provide adequate food, clothing, recreation and medical care;
- Freedom (for businesses) from unfair competition and domination by monopolies;
- The right of every family to a decent home and a good education;
- The right to adequate protection from the economic fears of old age, sickness, accident and unemployment;

It was not believed that our forefathers intended America to manage the world. That is not why people from all over came to America. They came to be free of tyranny and oppression and the freedom to practice their better intentions and make a better life for themselves and their children. Unfortunately, the dark side of our heritage also manifested a mistreatment and brutality in the form of indentured slavery of African, Chinese and Hispanic people and American Indians. With regard to these groups, their full civil and social respect has been a long and difficult struggle but there has been progress. As someone once said, "it's not so much in reaching the end of a journey but knowing you are heading in the right direction."

One could say that our global posture since the late '50s has been undermining what made this nation strong, including those constitutional principles that have been corrupted in U.S. efforts to prevail aggressively throughout the world. On the contrary, turning inward will actually make it easier for the United States to work out new relations with the other countries. Instead of dominating others, we can learn to live with differences. Instead of attacking foreign governments that deviate from the U.S. model, America can once again serve as a model of self-determination for all nations. In 1958, William J. Lederer gave us a heads-up lesson in American arrogance by writing his book, "The Ugly American," which showed how an overbearing foreign policy led to grave errors of judgment and foreign relations in Southeast Asia that we do not want to repeat again. Perhaps, aggression with guns and tanks and planes will give way to wars with cyberspace and technical intelligence. This means that our young people must be educated to meet those challenges.

In the last few decades, the U.S. economy has drifted further from the promises of the compassionate administrations, creating in its place a broad labor market of the underclass-temporary jobs paying unlivable wages and often filled with illegal immigrants. Guaranteed public jobs paying more than the minimum wage would permanently and automatically stabilize the economy, swelling the ranks of public workers in recessions and shrinking them when private jobs became abundant. Instead of punishing the working poor most severely in downturns, as the system now does, it would redistribute the costs to all taxpayers to share as a public obligation. Real jobs would mean that reliable incomes would flow into those underprivileged communities, providing a concrete basis for economic development and neighborhood restoration as well as the redemption of damaged lives. If the job slots included school-age young people and men and women in the bleakest circumstances they could suddenly become valued members of their families and the communities in which they would go to work producing real improvements while gaining for themselves a foothold on the economic ladder, If eligibility were linked to continuing their education, young people would get practical on-the-job training and a strong reason to stay in school. Even the American military could provide expertise in training young people. Old sergeants know how to take unpromising kids and turn them into highly competent and disciplined young people.

Starting in the 1920s, there was a philosophy of that era, improbable as it sounds today, that was known as corporate liberalism. General Electric was the leading exponent of the progressive-minded companies. Greider points out that during the 1920s, GE was a pioneer in developing workplace and community relations that defused the harsher conflicts of labor vs capital. Before the government became a social activist, General Electric was already experimenting with innovations like profit sharing and worker councils. Its CEO even articulated a vision that someday workers would become the company's owners as the majority shareholders. Cooperation, GE argued then, enhances efficiency and sustains profit and long-term prosperity. Other big names like Kodak, DuPont, General Motors, U.S. Steel and Standard Oil also supported various progressive measures. Collectively, these elements fashioned the informal understandings known as the social contract. Companies would provide their employees with job security; industrial wages that rose in step with productivity; and health insurance, pensions, and other benefits, and inclusive bargaining would be the means to settling disputes. Not everyone in the country benefited, but the industrial arrangement became the core model for the postwar economy and helped create the large and stable American middle class.

The concept of "corporate liberalism" that was prominent in the 1920s with some of the great corporations was to reconsider the employee morale by ensuring that everyone who works, whether in management or on the assembly line, deserved to "own" their work, i.e., to exercise personal responsibility for what they do and enjoy the mutual respect and the right to contribute and collaborate in making important decisions and share in the profits. These elements of voice and status are very important to personal satisfaction in one's work. The most progressive companies encourage the cooperative spirit from top to bottom. Most people take a great deal more care and responsibility when they have investment of ownership and that also applies to one's work. Numerous academic studies have shown and outstanding companies already understand that collaborative relationships between top management and the workforce are more productive and profitable. The profits are shared because the workers are also the owners.

Our history of unions in this country goes back to the 1800s and the Industrial Revolution when workers were highly exploited, giving rise to a more aggressive movement to unionize workers for their protection and decent treatment. The concept of labor-management relations had roots going back to the Protocol of Peace by Louis Brandeis in 1912 followed by the New York City garment workers' strike that same year. Later, in 1949 Dorothea de Scheinitz published her work on labor and management in a common effort to reach cooperative understandings.

Unfortunately, in the 1970s it all fell apart. Major companies began to break the truce with organized labor (largely due to the aggressive stand of Ronald Reagan regarding the Air Traffic Control Patco Union issue) and also turned hard against the government. The Business Roundtable and other groups, allied with hard-right ideologues, were taking command of the Republican Party. General Electric once again led the way, this time as the premier example of the harsh new bottom-line strategy that put corporations in conflict with workers and social values. Frank P. Doyle, GE executive vice president, acknowledged in retirement, "We did a lot of violence to the expectations of the American workforce." At that point, liberal Democrats might have reformed the regulatory system to make it more flexible. Instead, they retreated. With the election of Ronald Reagan in 1980, the old liberal order was over.

One of the dominant themes of the decades from the 1920s up through the 1970s had been the reversal of the historic role of unions, namely, steadily increasing wages and benefits in order to share in the company's productive profits. According to Bluestone and Harrison, the gains in living standards driven by unions had been made possible through comparable increases in productivity and the result was an overall reduction of inequality in society. Then starting in the early 1980s, an adversarial stance was taken by management to retrieve distributive gains that had been won by unions and their members over the years. Management used forcing and threatening strategies and was often prepared to use the threat of bankruptcy to gain the advantage. About that time, according to Daniel Di Salvo, assistant professor of political science at the City College of New York, wrote, "Government-workers' unions have been political juggernauts in the U.S. since the unseen collective- bargaining-rights revolution of the 1960s and 70s. These unions are different and more powerful than those that battle owners and managers in the private sector. To advance their interests, unions in the public sector have created cartels with their political allies, mostly in the Democratic Party, to the exclusion of the taxpaying public." In Daniel Di Salvo's book,

"Government Unions and the Bankrupting of America," he gives an excellent outline of how this aspect of a government takeover of public service happened and what can be done to protect the public interest.

On the private sector side, as we all know, corporations started to outsource factories and services and jobs to foreign countries thereby lowering their cost of labor. At the same time, management and higher positions in the corporations began giving themselves huge salaries, bonuses and "golden parachute" severances from the company. In the meantime, as mentioned at the beginning of this essay, the buying power of worker wages had not significantly improved over the last 25 years. On a more cynical note, one might think of what has been happening as the "rape of America."

A full-scale effort on the part of both private and public agencies must be waged through the willingness to invest in the future by creating the many jobs needed to reinforce our dilapidating infrastructure. As pointed out before, the vast investments made during WWII gave rise to the great economic recovery and sustained stability for many years. This must be accompanied by standards of equitable and cooperative participation in the direction, productivity and profits of our corporations.

One other concern of many Americans today in our modern society is the issue of Islamic immigration.

There have been books written about the "Infiltration" of seditious Islamic forces threatening our national security. I have heard and read reports that Europe and Western Civilization that was founded on Judeo-Christian religious principles are giving way to Muslim influences and Sharia law even though demographic studies show that France and Germany have the largest proportion of Muslims and that amounts to only seven and eight percent, respectively. It appears that there are concentrations of these cultural/religious groups much like other ethnic groups have formed in our own country. It is not unusual until generations that follow become assimilated and enculturated into the larger society. It is unreasonable, in my view, that a host nation would simply take a "live and let live" attitude while neglecting the establishment of social boundaries. In other words, it ought to be established that those who have come as immigrants respect the laws and culture of the host country. When Americans go to live in an Arab country it is expected that the Americans must respect the laws and customs of that country. It is only common courtesy if nothing else.

There are divisions among the Islamic people–the Shia and the Sunni sects. In terms of leadership, the Shia hold that leadership must come by inheritance directly from Mohammed while the Sunni, which represent 85% of the Islam population, take the position that leadership must be earned by proving oneself worthy and capable. These bifurcations are not uncommon. When you look at traditional Roman and Byzantine Catholic and then Roman Catholic and Protestant–Jewish Orthodox and Jewish Reform, even political divisions of reactionary conservative and radical liberal, there is an obvious tendency on the part of human nature to want to stay close to the familiar and traditional, on the one hand, and the desire to move forward on the other. There have been militant elements in Judeo/Christianity as in the Crusades and the Inquisition which was sanctioned by the Papacy. One could also point to justification in the Bible for those cruel persuasions and bloody seekers of martyrdom. My sense is that in Islam, the militancy movement is on a much smaller scale than was the barbarism of the early Church. I am not persuaded that Islamic leadership is dedicated to the destruction of Western Civilization although there are elements that do–just as early Christianity sought to Christianize the world. Perhaps, Islam, being a younger religion, is also going through stages of evolution that Christianity has gone through. Reza Aslan, in his book, "No god but God" points out how different sects have interpreted the Koran in different ways regarding how men must treat women. One interpretation is demeaning and punitive while another is more considerate and respectful. In another book by Irshad Manji titled, "The Trouble with Islam Today," she is urging those of her religion to reform the faith, empower women, encourage independent thinking and respect for the views of others.

So where are the roots of our political woes? In my view, the fate of our future lies in the quality of parent/child relationships and good learning experiences. Those of us who have studied Political Science and History as well as Psychology can see that if a child is treated kindly and with respect for his own personhood as he/she is growing up, that person will feel good about themselves and be inclined to move forward into the world with confidence and good will while, on the other hand, if the child grows up without positive regard or is an object of abuse of one kind or another, that child is likely to carry over its perception of the world as hostile and unfriendly and must, in adulthood, elect to take on the extraordinary challenges and struggles to correct faulty learning and experience or become an incompetent liability to others. In the latter situation, the child who does not feel good about him or herself will likely either turn against the self or others in some malignant way—and, in either case, that person will become a wasted human resource and be costly to the world at large. Our prisons and psychiatric wards are glutted with such individuals—not to mention those who plague the world with colossal exploitations. When seen on a scale of extremes, we can note the brutal, exploitive, narcissistic bully or the self-defeating unproductive and unhappy recluse on the one hand or the cooperative, friendly and contributing member of society who raises healthy, happy and productive children on the other. On a lesser scale of extremism, we can see those of a political persuasion who favor or perhaps need to stay on familiar ground toward the traditions of the past or those who are more emboldened to seek new adventures and knowledge. The social, economic, and political community, therefore, must be capable of providing a government that enables all people within that society the security it needs in order to pursue its better intentions.

To conclude, I would like to present a few more ideas toward a reformation of our political-economic society:

We, the Friends of the Republic say:

- In the future large corporations, or small ones should be held responsible for the consequences of their failures. We all have to learn from our mistakes.
- The Federal government ought to be reduced to only the functions of national defense, inter-state commerce and social security. Furthermore, if all the money in taxes sent to Washington to pay for all the other government functions and bureaucracies were kept at the State level, there would likely be enough to provide free education up through the university level and free medical services for all the citizens of the State as well as enough funds to provide for those unable to care for themselves. This is necessary to insure a viable and self-enhancing society.
- There ought to be standards of social conscience and professional competence established for

anyone who aspires to serve in public office. A Democratic Republic is a wonderful form of government but it does have its limitations if the quality and character of the leadership is wanting.

- There must be penalties for anyone who does not exercise their civic responsibility and cast their vote. When we see what people in less fortunate countries do to make sure their votes are recognized, it makes us feel rather dismayed at the lack of enthusiasm of our own people.

- The executive branch of the government has become so over-burdened with gigantic responsibilities and complexities that we ought to consider having two Chief Executives; one for foreign affairs who has some expertise and experience in that area and the other for domestic affairs who has demonstrated competencies and understanding of those kinds of responsibilities. In addition, we might have a Board of individuals at the top who are chosen to represent the character and integrity of this country's ideals of honesty, fair play and good sportsmanship. The ethics and moral standards of our country in business and industry have been so dissimulated that our children hardly know what this nation stands for anymore.

- Our leaders could become a bit humbler and more circumspect so that we might learn from those in other countries who have done better than we in such areas as medical services. In an interview on the Fareed Zacaria program, a guest who had studied medical services around the world had discovered that Switzerland has had a health service system very similar to what is called "Obama Care" for the past 18 years and it is working beautifully for virtually all the people and at a much lower cost than ours. They call their system a medical service. We call our medical insurance and that is because it is a competitive industry and much more expensive. It, therefore, must serve the financial interests of the share and stockholders.

- Lobbyists in Washington wield too much influence on the Congress and serve only the purposes of the large corporations. They are able to spend a great deal more money than most of us have to spend on fortifying of their own special interests. This puts a great disadvantage over those of the middle class–the backbone of America–and those who have been elected by the people to represent them in a fair and equitable manner.

- The income tax issue is a vexing one and deeply offends those of us who must pay large amounts of money to someone else to figure out how much we must pay the government because it has become much too complicated for even those of us who are well educated professional people to do it ourselves. It is also grossly unfair for the average working-class individual to pay more income tax than those endowed with exorbitant wealth and financial benefits. In 2012, Warren Buffett sent a message to Congress advising making suitable changes to the federal tax law stating that his secretary paid more income tax than he.

- One of the major keystones of any healthy, progressive, and competitive society is education. In terms of priorities, it should come before sports and entertainment because of its ultimate value in preserving and advancing the viability of future generations of Americans. Education should not be politicized or bureaucratized, but regarded as a true profession and those that enter it ought to be regarded with standards of excellence the norm. Education insures the viability and competitiveness of the nation in perpetuity.

- Our country is suffering from a lack of talented and capable leadership because of the political aspirants indebted for the exceptional financial contributions of a few. Furthermore, running for another term detracts from the time and energy an elected official ought to be spending at his job. It does seem to many of us that the broadcasting companies ought to be prevailed upon to donate some airtime to a worthy prospective aspirant for public office since they are supported by sponsors that gain from the public consumer.

- In view of the fact that people are living much longer than they were when Social Security was established, it would be better for all of us if the retirement age was boosted up to 70 with early retirement an option at 68. Furthermore, part-time continued employment could be established as a normal pattern and that would allow those who have gained so much experience and skill in a particular occupation to pass on to younger employees and those newly entering the market place the benefit of what the elder people have learned. Another consideration is the fact that much of production and services are being provided by workers overseas, robotics and home office employment. It seems feasible, therefore, that the work hours be shortened so people can have more time to enjoy their families and for recreation.

- The issue of gun control in the U.S. is one of grave importance. According to Wikipedia sources (in the year 2000), there were 52,447 deaths deliberately caused by firearms and 23,237 accidental deaths caused by firearms. According to the CDC/National Center for injury prevention and control, the U.S. death rate from firearms in 2003 was eight times higher than its counterparts in other parts of the world. We ought to realize that when this issue was considered by framers of our Constitution, people lived in outlying and isolated farms and were vulnerable to attacks from outlaws, Indians, wild animals, and even British sympathizers. It made sense for people who lived in those times to have some way of defending themselves. Today, however, we live in a civilized society protected by police forces and legal prohibitions—at least this is what is intended. We must take firearms (and especially those that are intended for war) out of the hands of those who are incapable of handling them responsibly—or at least, as Senator Moynihan once said in 1993, if we can't control guns, at least let us tax bullets and ammunition or set standards on who is allowed to purchase them. The other alternative, as suggested by John R. Lott, Jr. in his 1998 publication "More Guns-Less Crime," is to legally allow all citizens to carry firearms as a protection against those who would be a threat. Do we really want to live in a gun toting society?

- Finally, the beauty of our system is that our forefathers understood that nothing is perfect so they designed our form of government to be changeable and improvable as the knowledge and awareness of the people evolves and grows. It is based on the premise that reasonable people of goodwill can sit down together with differing views and persuasions and talk sensibly about a consensual course of action for the betterment of all. With the sincere input of the leaders, one can determine which confluence of ideas will likely give the best results for the needed choices and directions.

In addition, we do not want to omit the wise recommendations of Warren Buffet who, in a recent interview with CNBC, offered persuasive reform measures in his Congressional Reform Act of 2012 as follows:

No tenure/no pension: Congress men and women collect a salary while in office and receive no pay when they are out of office.

Congress (past, present & future) participates in Social Security: All funds in the Congressional retirement fund move to the Social Security system immediately. All future funds flow into the Social Security system, and Congress participates with the American people. It may not be used for any other purpose. Congress can purchase their own retirement plan, just as all Americans do.

Congress will no longer vote themselves a pay raise. Congressional pay will rise by the lower of CPI or 3%.

Congress will lose their current health care system. They must participate in the same health care system as the American people. Congress must equally abide by all laws they impose on the American people.

All contracts with past and present Congressmen and women are void effective 12/1/12. The American people did not make these contracts with Congressmen or women. Congress made all these contracts with themselves.

Serving in Congress is an honor, not a career. The Founding Fathers envisioned citizen legislators, so ours should serve their term(s), then go home and back to work.

Isn't it time we cleaned house and thought about new guidelines for our country's future? Let's all express our thoughts and feelings to the politicians in Washington and let them know the will of the people.

BIBLIOGRAPHY

Aslan, Reza (2006), <u>No god but God:</u> The Origins, Evolution and Future of Islam, New York, Random House, Inc.

Baker, Russ (2009), <u>Family of Secrets</u>; The Bush Dynasty, The Powerful Forces That Put It In The White House, and What Their Influence Means For America, New York, Bloomsbury Press

Beven, Gerald; translator (2003), <u>Alexis de Tocqueville. Democracy in America:</u> New York, Penguin Classics

Blackmon, Douglas A. (2008), <u>Slavery by Another Name</u>; The Re-Enslavement of Black Americans from the Civil War to World War Il, New York Anchor Books

Bork, Robert H. (1996), <u>Slouching Toward Gomorrah;</u> Modern Liberalism And American Decline, New York, Regan Books

Bradley, Bill (2007), <u>The New American Story:</u> New York, Random House

Brzezinski, Zbigniew (2012), <u>Strategic Vision;</u> New York, Basic Books

Buchanan, Patrick J. (2006), <u>State of Emergency:</u> The Third World Invasion and Conquest of America, New York, Thomas Dunne Books

Coontz, Stephanie (1992). <u>The Way We Never Were•</u> American Families and the Nostalgia Trap, New York, Basic Books

DiSalvo, Daniel (2011), <u>Government Unions and the Bankruptcy of America.</u> New York, Encounter Books

Donald, David Herbert (1995), <u>Lincoln</u>; New York, Simon& Schuster

Dorgan, Senator Byron L. (2006), <u>Take This Job and Ship It:</u> How Corporate Greed and Brain Dead Politics Are Selling Out America, New York,

Thomas Dunn Books Draut, Tamara (2005), <u>Strapped;</u> Why America's 20- and 30-Somethings Can't Get Ahead, New York, Doubleday

Dray, Philip (2010), <u>There is Power in a Union•</u> New York, First Anchor Books Ellis, Joseph J. (2007), <u>American Creation</u>; New York, Alfred A. Knoff

Erikson, Erik (1950), <u>Childhood and Society;</u> New York, W.W. Norton& Co.

Fisk, Robert (2007), <u>The Great War for Civilizatiorr</u> The Conquest of the Middle East, New York, Vantage Press

Freddoso, David (2008), <u>The Case Against Barak Obama:</u> The Unlikely Rise and Unexamined Agenda of the Media's Favorite Candidate, Washington DC, Regnery Publishing Co.

Friedman, Thomas L. (2005), <u>The World Is Flat•</u> A Brief History ofthe 21 st Century, New York, Farrar, Straus and Giroux

Frost, S. E., Jr. (1989), <u>Basic Teachings of the Great Philosophers;</u> New York, Anchor Books

Gingrich, Newt (2008), <u>Real Change;</u> From The World That Fails to The World That Works, Regnery Publishing Co. New York, Warner Books, Inc.

Gabriel, Brigitte (2006), <u>Because They Hate:</u> A Survivor of Islamic Terror Warns America, New York, St. Martin's Press

Goodwin, Doris Kearns (1994), <u>No Ordinary Time</u>; Franklin and Eleanor Roosevelt: The Home Front in WWII, New York, Simon& Schuster Paperback

Greider, William (2009), <u>Come Home. America</u>; The Rise and Fall and Redeeming Promise) of Our Country, New York, Rodale, Inc.

Iococca, Lee (2007), <u>Where Have All The Leaders Gone?</u>: New York, Scribner, Inc.

Iserbyt, Charlotte Thomson (1999), <u>The Dumbing Down of America:</u> Ravenna, Ohio, Conscience Press

Johnston, David Cay (2008), <u>Free Lunch</u>: How the Wealthiest Americans Enrich Themselves at Government Expense (and stick you with the bill); Penguin Group

Kennan, George F. (1972), <u>Memoirs 1950-1963</u>• New York, Pantheon Books

Lederer, William J. and Burdick, Eugene (1965), <u>The Ugly American:</u> New York, W.W. Norton& Co. Paperback

Lott, John R., Jr. (1998), <u>More Guns Less Crime</u>• Understanding Crime and Gun Control Laws, Chicago, University of Chicago Press

Manji, Irshad (2003), <u>The Trouble with Islam Today:</u> New York, St. Martin's Press

McCullough, David (2005), <u>1776</u>• New York, Simon& Shuster

McGreal, Ian P., Edited by, <u>Great Thinkers of the Western World</u>; The major ideas and classic works of more than 100 outstanding Western philosophers, physical and social scientists, psychologists, religious writers, and theologians, New York, NY, HarperCollins Publishers, Inc.

Moyers, Bill (2011), <u>Bill Movers Journal</u>; New York, The New Press

Nolte, Dorothy Law (1998), <u>Children Learn What They Live:</u> New York, Workman Publishing Company, Inc.

Obama, Barak (2008), <u>Change You Can Believe In:</u> New York, Three Rivers Press Obama, Barak (2006), <u>The Audacity of Hope:</u> New York, Crown Publishers Obama, Barak (1995), <u>Dreams from My Father:</u> New York, Broadway Paperbacks

Roberts, J.M. (1993), <u>A Short History of the World:</u> New York, Oxford University

Smith, Adam (2009), <u>The Wealth of Nations</u>• A Digireads.Com Book

Spencer, Robert (2008), <u>Stealth Jihad</u>• How Radical Islam is Subverting America, Washington, DC, Regnery Publishing, Inc.

Sperry, Paul (2005), <u>Infiltration</u>• How Muslim Spies and Subversives Have Penetrated Washington, Nashville, Tennessee, Nelson Current

Tanenhaus, Sam (2009), <u>The Death of Conservatism</u>• A Movement and its Consequences, New York, Random House

Taylor, Maxwell D., General of the Army (1972), <u>Swords and Plowshares</u>• A Memoir, New York, De Capo Press

Tett, Gillian (2009), <u>Fool's Gold</u> How the Bold Dream of a Small Tribe at J.P. Morgan was Corrupted by Wall Street Greed and Unleashed a Catastrophe; New York, Free Press

Thompson, Nicholas (2009), <u>The Hawk and the Dove</u>• Paul Nitze, George Kennan, and the History of the Cold War, New York, Henry Holt& Co.

Thoreau, Henry David (1993), <u>Walden and Other Writings:</u> New York, Barnes& Noble, Inc.

Updike, John (2006), <u>Terrorist</u> New York, Alfred A. Knopf Webb, Jim (2008), <u>A Time to Fight:</u> New York, Broadway Books

Wills, Garry (2010), <u>Bomb Power</u> The Modern Presidency and the National Security State, New York, The Penguin Press